T0248422

Praise for *The Succe~~ss~~...*

"Managing a successful hybrid team is not easy and requires a strategy and plan to make it work. This guide shares a very practical step -by-step roadmap to attract, nurture and retain a world class team that delivers outstanding business value and success. Full of really useful examples and interesting facts, this book is a must have for any leader working in a hybrid environment or even if you just want to build a stronger team."

—Georgina Owens,
CTO and Non Executive Director

"For the past 20 years I've lived in, led and built teams in companies of all sizes. Perrine's detailed and organized research and organization work puts so much of real life experience into a practical one-stop-shop. I recommend this book as a must read for anyone wanting to lead a hybrid team, and would even extend to any team, but wondering how."

—Sylvain Querne,
CEO, 6sicuro.it (Howden group)

"*The Successful Hybrid Team* is the book every modern leader needs. This guide takes us on a step-by-step journey to learn how to lead a world-class team in hybrid work. There is a revolution happening at work. It is bigger than the introduction of emails, and bigger than cloud adoption. It is called hybrid work and it is changing the way teams work in a post-COVID economy through new technologies and social dynamics. Only the teams that are mastering culture are thriving in hybrid work. In this insightful new book from acclaimed workplace expert Perrine Farque, readers are taken on an in-depth journey into how to build world-class hybrid teams that produce great results consistently through fostering a strong culture."

—**Garry Ridge,**
The Culture Coach,
CEO & Chairman WD-40 Company

"As a CEO managing people based in Atlanta, Florida, Romania, Philippines and many more locations, reading *The Successful Hybrid Team* was a gift! The book felt like it was written for me and I know there are countless other people like me who will feel the same way. Phenomenal work Perrine. This book will be required reading for my people managers! If you are looking for real world examples and actionable insights into building a successful team in remote work or hybrid work, look no further, this book is for you!

—**David Feldman,**
WSJ and USA Today Bestselling Author
and Founder of 3 Owl Agency

"If you are looking for ways to build a strong corporate culture in a hybrid environment, Perrine Farque has cracked the code. With a proven four pillar framework, she explains how you can proactively foster a workplace where people feel connected, not just through technology but with each other. If you are wondering how leading hybrid organizations are making it work, pick up this book and wonder no more."

—**Karin M. Reed,**
award-winning author of "On-Camera Coach",
"Suddenly Virtual" and "Suddenly Hybrid"

"As a leader with 30+ years experience managing teams and people, I have always researched ways to build and nurture the best teams. Managing teams is always a challenge, especially when team members are remote or working in different countries. *The Successful Hybrid Team: What the Best Hybrid Teams Know About Culture that Others Don't (But Wish They Did)* is the perfect book for any manager, leader and team leader who wants to build and nurture a world-class team that is remote or spread across different countries. I could not recommend this book enough!"

—**Andy Santacroce,**
a 30+ year experienced technology leader

"Our world changed over the last 2 years, and it will never be the same again – inevitably you are managing people today in a way that none of our predecessors have had the experience of. This must-read, The Successful Hybrid Team, will enable you to create the right culture in a remote work environment and is the missing piece for today's leaders. It is the in-depth analysis of topics like how to best leverage meetings in a hybrid environment, what most common pitfalls are for those leading hybrid teams and how to avoid them that are helping me on a daily (if not hourly!) basis. I have already found the checklists at the end an essential resource making this book meaningful, useful and impactful!"

—**Andrew Macadam,**
CEO of WI.HN

The Successful Hybrid Team

What the Best Hybrid Teams Know About Culture That Others Don't (But Wish They Did)

Perrine Farque

WILEY

This edition first published 2023

Copyright © 2023 by John Wiley & Sons, Ltd.

Registered office

John Wiley & Sons Ltd, The Atrium, Southern Gate, Chichester, West Sussex, PO19 8SQ, United Kingdom

For details of our global editorial offices, for customer services and for information about how to apply for permission to reuse the copyright material in this book please see our website at www.wiley.com.

All rights reserved. No part of this publication may be reproduced, stored in a retrieval system, or transmitted, in any form or by any means, electronic, mechanical, photocopying, recording or otherwise, except as permitted by the UK Copyright, Designs and Patents Act 1988, without the prior permission of the publisher. Wiley publishes in a variety of print and electronic formats and by print-on-demand. Some material included with standard print versions of this book may not be included in e-books or in print-on-demand. If this book refers to media such as a CD or DVD that is not included in the version you purchased, you may download this material at http://booksupport.wiley.com. For more information about Wiley products, visit www.wiley.com.

Designations used by companies to distinguish their products are often claimed as trademarks. All brand names and product names used in this book are trade names, service marks, trademarks or registered trademarks of their respective owners. The publisher is not associated with any product or vendor mentioned in this book. Limit of Liability/Disclaimer of Warranty: While the publisher and author have used their best efforts in preparing this book, they make no representations or warranties with respect to the accuracy or completeness of the contents of this book and specifically disclaim any implied warranties of merchantability or fitness for a particular purpose. It is sold on the understanding that the publisher is not engaged in rendering professional services and neither the publisher nor the author shall be liable for damages arising here from. If professional advice or other expert assistance is required, the services of a competent professional should be sought.

Library of Congress Cataloging-in-Publication Data

Names: Farque, Perrine, author.

Title: The successful hybrid team : what the best hybrid teams know about culture that others don't (but wish they did) / Perrine Farque.

Description: Chichester, West Sussex, United Kingdom : John Wiley & Sons, 2023. | Includes bibliographical references and index.

Identifiers: LCCN 2022031877 (print) | LCCN 2022031878 (ebook) | ISBN 9781119888550 (paperback) | ISBN 9781119888567 (adobe pdf) | ISBN 9781119888574 (epub)

Subjects: LCSH: Virtual work teams. | Flexible work arrangements. | Corporate culture. | Business communication. | Organizational change.

Classification: LCC HD66 .F35 2023 (print) | LCC HD66 (ebook) | DDC 658.4/022—dc23/eng/20220831

LC record available at https://lccn.loc.gov/2022031877

LC ebook record available at https://lccn.loc.gov/2022031878

Cover Design: Wiley

Cover Image: © elenabsl/Shutterstock

Author photo: Courtesy of Perrine Farque

SKY10035996_090922

CONTENTS

CONTENTS

INTRODUCTION

This book's journey started a long time ago, in a classroom in a small town called Dole, in France. When I was in primary school, from age six to age eleven, I was extremely shy and spent a lot of time observing my classmates. As I was watching my friends work on school projects in groups, I noticed how certain groups of children seemed to always complete their class projects on time, while others were always late or needed help from the teacher. At the time, I didn't really understand why this happened, but I was certainly very interested in these dynamics.

A few years later, as I started university, me and my fellow students often had to work in groups to complete work assignments that were part of our curriculum. Again, I quickly noticed that these research projects were completed earlier and scored better grades when completed by certain groups of students, while other groups of students were often late and scored lower grades. I wasn't quite sure what 'magic' made some teams work better than others, but I was fascinated by my observations. The best teams were not just made up of smarter students; in fact, some of the best teams had some students that were only average as individuals. Likewise, some of the worst performing teams had some excellent students in them, so a team's success was not linked to the quality of each individual.

Shortly after university, I started working for a few technology companies in London, and I was curious to see if companies had figured out how to make all teams perform well at the same time. Instead, I was shocked to see that each team had their own way of operating and that each department could produce completely different results from one another, with some exceeding their targets and some struggling with their targets. For example, in one company, which was a software vendor, the sales team had not hit the sales target for the last three quarters and had a high employee turnover; in contrast, the software engineering team consistently shipped new software updates and new software features on time, with excellent customer feedback and almost no employee attrition. These differences in team performance from one team to another were consistent among all organizations I worked with. When I asked around as to what management principles managers were using, I only received vague answers, and it appeared that most managers and team leaders were not following any specific method.

Although I learnt a few principles about team management during my time working for technology organizations, I still felt like something was missing in the way people were being managed. I continued to work for a few other technology companies and went on to watch team after team never quite reach their full potential. Some of the teams I worked for had a very difficult culture, whereby team members, including myself, didn't feel safe to contribute to new ideas without fear of being ridiculed or penalized.

At that point, it became clear to me that I should start my own firm offering consultations to organizations and speak about a method to improve team management. As I started receiving an increasing number of requests for consultations with regard to team management and culture, I realized that the demand for creating better workplaces where teams and organizations thrive was very strong. During the first year, I received many messages from employees who were feeling disengaged at work and disconnected from their team, excluded by their boss, or even considering leaving their organization. I also received many requests from managers who confessed that they didn't know how to create the right environment for their people to thrive.

It was becoming clear that there was a real need for better team management systems, so I decided to write a book focusing on inclusion in the workplace, and I had many speaking engagements on that topic. Demand for my work exceeded my expectations as I started to speak more globally, including for firms headquartered in North America, Europe, and even Asia. Then Covid-19 happened. The Covid pandemic created a revolution in the workplace. It was bigger than the introduction of emails, and bigger than cloud adoption: it is called 'hybrid work', and it changed the way teams function in a post-Covid economy through new technologies and social dynamics. Only the teams that are mastering culture are thriving in hybrid work. I became convinced that I should write a book to help team managers learn how to build world-class hybrid teams that produce great results consistently through fostering a strong culture.

Unlike my previous book, this one focuses on how to make a team successful in a hybrid work environment by focusing on the culture element. Over the past 18 months, I have observed what successful teams do to consistently perform well in a flexible work environment, with some team members working from home, some team members working in the office, and some team members alternating between the two. I have worked very closely with many clients, and together we have identified a certain framework that makes a team successful when working in a distributed environment. All the learnings that I share in this book are based on my own observations, having worked with hundreds of people working in teams since the start of Covid-19. 'I also share observations on what makes the best teams succeed in a hybrid work environment, drawn from my experience of working in a flexible working environment during my own career, and what I have learned from a few years of working in hybrid teams.

My sincere hope is that you enjoy reading this book and you find some helpful strategies that will help you build, nurture, and retain a world-class team in a hybrid work environment. Ultimately, my goal is to help create workplaces where people and organizations thrive. Whether you are a CEO, HR professional, team leader, or entrepreneur, and whether you work at a small business, mid-size organization, or large enterprise, my wish is that this book will help you to build the world-class team that you are capable of building, and create a workplace where your people and your organization are successful and productive.

My Personal Journey as a Multicultural Digital Nomad

As I started writing this book, I reflected on my own journey and what led me to write about what makes a team successful when it is geographically distributed. In many ways, my personal and professional journey has given me a lot of experience that is extremely relevant to this book. To start with, I have a history of living in different countries and speaking different languages. As a child, I grew up in France, and I spent most of my summer holidays in Germany, speaking German and hanging out with our German friends. My dad had kept in touch with his German friend from school, and each summer I would spend a few weeks in Germany, learning the local culture and getting to know the German lifestyle. In my early adulthood, I moved to Italy, where I spent three years working at a company in Genoa. I learnt the Italian language, I discovered Italian culture, and I also moved in with an Italian man, who eventually became my husband. In time, I moved to the United Kingdom (London), where I got to practice my English language; I also learnt the British culture, and I became familiar with the British way of life. Having lived and worked in three different countries, I quickly learnt that to be successful at working with people from different cultures, it is critical to have a strong cultural awareness. If I had been behaving with my London team the same way I had been behaving with my team in Genoa, I would not have been as successful. The unwritten rules of culture play a key role in how teams communicate, give and receive feedback, and perform.

The second experience that has helped me write this book is that I have worked for many years 'on the road'. As a head of marketing, I was often managing tradeshow and industry event sponsorship and presence for my employers, meaning that I was frequently travelling for work, out of the office for several days at a time. These business trips, which were often abroad, meant working remotely, and I learnt how to successfully work with a team even when in a different location. The challenges of working from different locations are not the same as for those working in the same office. For instance, remote workers are missing out on a lot of 'water cooler conversations' that happen organically in the office, and as a result, they tend to be less aware of the dynamics around decisions. To an extent, remote workers must work twice as hard to communicate with different stakeholders to keep up with the unofficial dynamics. Because most decisions taken in the organization are the result of multiple, unofficial chats that tend to happen face-to-face, in between meetings, remote workers must work hard to stay in the know of all the water cooler chats. In many ways, working remotely for so long has taught me strategies that I now use to build successful teams in a hybrid work environment. A lot of this is down to education and awareness and is about teaching managers practical steps to create the right environment for a world-class hybrid team.

My hope is that my personal and professional experiences as a multicultural digital nomad will help you uncover how to manage your distributed team successfully. It is my goal that managers, HR professionals, entrepreneurs, and business leaders attract, nurture, and retain the best talent for their distributed teams by putting culture at the centre of everything they do, so that people and organizations thrive in a hybrid world.

1 The World of Work Is Changing Faster than Ever Before

There was a Time Before Emails. . .

In 1965, the first emails were sent from computers at the Massachusetts Institute of Technology (MIT). Each user's message was added to a local file called 'MAIL BOX'. The proposed uses of the proto-email system were for communication to notify users that files had been backed up.[1]

Prior to emails, workers would spend their mornings going through a pile of handwritten memos and notes from co-workers and notes from phone messages left by an assistant. They would then respond by writing down (yes, handwriting!) lengthy replies, send them via mail, and then wait approximately seven days for a response. At that time, messages were official, formally written, and left no place for mistakes. The decision-making process was therefore much longer. When emails were first introduced in 1965 and then widely adopted in the workplace in the 1970s, the business world went through the first revolution. Suddenly, teams could communicate instantly and discuss group projects at a much faster pace, and the transmission of information between co-workers reached a new era. The use of rapid one-to-many delivery increased the amount of communication colleagues had, as compared to the era immediately preceding the widespread use of email. According to Statista, roughly 306.4 billion emails were estimated to have been sent and received each day in 2020, and this figure is expected to increase to over 376.4 billion daily mails by 2025.[2]

In the early 2000s, emails at work became omnipresent. With the adoption of the BlackBerry in 2003 and its portability, professionals were expected to check their work emails and answer messages immediately, even after working hours. The impact on teamwork was significant; colleagues had to learn how to respond to a never-ending influx of messages from their co-workers coming through their inbox, from morning until evening and even during the weekend. Employees also had to quickly adapt to new expectations and be available much more rapidly to respond to requests. With that came a new etiquette regarding work emails, ranging from when to send emails and what tone to use with a co-worker (the shift from formal to informal happened organically), to how to start an email, how to end an email, who to copy and who not to copy, etc.

The Second Workplace Revolution: Cloud Computing

It's hard to pinpoint exactly when cloud technologies were widely adopted in the workplace. In the 1990s, many personal computers were connected to cloud technologies as the tools became more affordable. Cloud technologies gained popularity in the late 1990s, when companies gained a better understanding of what it did for them. In simple terms, cloud computing refers to storing and accessing data and programs over the internet as opposed to a computer's hard drive. Common examples of cloud computing include Dropbox, Salesforce, and Webex. According to ZDNet, some of the top cloud providers in 2021 include AWS, Microsoft Azure and Google Cloud.[3] Saying that the adoption of cloud computing has changed the world of work is an understatement. Many workers started working from home thanks to the adoption of cloud computing; the use of the company's resources was now possible outside of the office. In addition to working remotely, workers could also communicate via new technologies, such as Skype, Gotomeeting, and Slack. This allowed for easy meetings with people in various locations, as well

Cloud computing technologies allowed workers to work from anywhere, at any time, how they wanted. It gave workers the freedom and autonomy to take control of their work. This shifted the traditional authority dynamics from the legacy office worker who was much more dependent on the manager's direction.

as group chats, channels for project discussions and updates, easy file sharing, and much more. The main shift that cloud computing brought to the workplace was the 'always-on' mindset it created.

The power was given to the workers with the adoption of cloud computing.

Figure 1.1   The second workplace revolution: cloud computing.

Covid-19 and the Third Workplace Revolution: Hybrid Work

For many people, the Covid-19 pandemic has widely transformed the way they work. Working from home became widely adopted overnight by the majority of knowledge workers globally in March 2020. One of my clients told me that he received an email from his CEO saying that every employee had to take all their belongings home, including their laptop, as they were going to work from home for an undefined period of time. That day would be the last day he saw his office for 18 months. It is hard to explain to anyone who has not experienced this what it was like. Many workers found themselves having to work from their home for the first time. Although the potential of working from home is concentrated among highly skilled knowledge workers among specific industries and roles, it remains a trend that is here to stay and is transforming most industries' workplaces. In many ways, the Covid-19 pandemic has removed the cultural and technological barriers that prevented hybrid work. Today's knowledge workers are living through a radical shift in professional life.

New technologies mean that even some traditional sectors, such as hospitality, are undergoing radical changes. Working from home will boost productivity by 4.8% as the post-Covid economy takes shape, according to a recent study of more than 30 000 US employees co-authored by José María Barrero of Instituto Tecnológico Autónomo de México and others.[4] Much of that comes from a reduced commuting time. Many workplace experts are positively associating the shift to hybrid work with an increase in productivity. Different studies demonstrate the correlation between hybrid work and productivity, with different explanations; some

attribute the increase in productivity to the increase in
working time due to the limited time spent commuting,
while some attribute it to happier staff who are more
efficient. Many employees who became remote workers
during the pandemic reported having more time for
creative-thinking during the time they would normally
spend on commuting. Employers responded to the new
hybrid work trend with different approaches. Some
traditional employers made the news because of their
conservative approach: Morgan Stanley's chief executive
told US staff to be back in the office.[5] JP Morgan also asked
employees to return to their offices during the pandemic.[6]
Even employers that come from less conservative industries
have asked their employees to return to the office, as is the
case with Google, who wanted its people back in the office.[7]
After nearly two years of the pandemic, many employers
and employees seem to agree that working from the office a
few days a week is the right balance. If we look at the
category of employees who have the option to choose
between working from home or working from their office,
studies have revealed that it's mostly educated workers
that have this option.[8] However, remote work has
also allowed more diverse workers from under-
represented groups to access the workplace. From
mothers with childcare duties, to employees living
in remote locations, to disabled employees, more
workers from

Finally, the shift to
hybrid work and remote
work has forced
employers to figure out
how to build a culture of
trust. When companies
had to send their
employees working from
home overnight,
employers suddenly had
to learn how to trust
their people.

under-represented groups now have gained access to the workplace, thanks to hybrid work and remote work.

Team leaders, managers, and CEOs suddenly had to find ways to build a culture of trust and psychological safety to continue to work together whilst being geographically distributed. Over time, teams that have nurtured a positive culture of psychological safety have enjoyed better relationships, stronger collaboration, improved teamwork, and better performance in hybrid work. The Covid-19 pandemic has significantly transformed the way we work and pushed the limits of what we believed was possible when working together in a remote or hybrid workplace', or similar. Whilst many team leaders, managers, and CEOs are still working out how to build successful teams in a highly distributed environment, the trend of hybrid work is here to stay and is forcing everyone to find ways of working well together in hybrid teams.

Endnotes

1. https://en.wikipedia.org/wiki/History_of_email

2. https://www.statista.com/statistics/456500/daily-number-of-e-mails-worldwide/

3. https://www.zdnet.com/article/the-top-cloud-providers-of-2021-aws-microsoft-azure-google-cloud-hybrid-saas/

4. https://www.business-standard.com/article/current-affairs/the-hybrid-work-revolution-after-covid-19-is-already-transforming-economies-121082700181_1.html

5. https://www.theguardian.com/business/2021/jun/15/morgan-stanley-boss-tells-us-staff-to-be-back-in-office-in-september

6. https://www.forbes.com/sites/jackkelly/2021/04/28/jp-morgan-requires-employees-to-return-to-their-offices-by-july-striking-a-blow-to-the-remote-work-trend/?sh=7314fc524cdc

7. https://www.bloomberg.com/news/articles/2021-07-15/google-googl-wants-employees-to-return-to-office-despite-productivity-gains

8. https://www.mckinsey.com/featured-insights/future-of-work/whats-next-for-remote-work-an-analysis-of-2000-tasks-800-jobs-and-nine-countries

2 Why a Culture of Belonging Is Key in Hybrid Work

Building Belonging Is Harder in Hybrid Work

Employees who work from the office are more likely to feel like they belong to a team. When you share the same space as your co-workers, you are more likely to share a personal story with them, to share a coffee, to share a moment with them, and to build a connection. When you work from home, these moments of connection do not happen organically or spontaneously, and it is harder to feel connected and like we belong to a team. Being in the office, we can easily have lunch with a co-worker or go to their desk to ask a question; when I worked in an office in pre-pandemic times, I would always start my day with some ice-breaker conversations with people sitting next to me. We would talk about our commute to work, about any story that happened on our morning commute, about our plans for the weekend; these simple conversations made me feel connected and close to my co-workers. Some of the top issues reported by employees who work remotely include an increased sense of isolation, a lack of social connection, an 'us versus them' mentality, and even a fear of missing out (FOMO). Some symptoms associated with isolation include increased stress levels, burnout, and feelings of exclusion. Some have even called this phenomenon 'the belonging tax'.

> For employees working remotely or in a hybrid environment, the belonging tax is the price they pay for the flexibility and convenience of working remotely.

At the organizational level, the belonging tax equates to a drop in employee engagement due to a drop in the employee experience, which could lead to lower job satisfaction. Managing employees in hybrid work is a balancing act. According to research carried out in 2021 by Canadian-based partners, inclusive workplace learning company Dialectic, and intranet software platform Jostle, 82% of remote workers report communication obstacles, and 83% report feeling disconnected from their workplace culture.[1] Indeed, some of the challenges of hybrid work and remote work include different access to information (informal post-meeting debrief in the office), to communication channels (around the water cooler), as well as more difficulties regarding relationship building, networking, and connection. While there are some great benefits linked to hybrid work for workers (think better work–life balance, more freedom, more convenience), employees working remotely or partly remotely report among the lowest levels of belonging within their organization. Ever since the post-pandemic world has appeared, more hybrid work employees are feeling left behind in terms of connection compared to their peers returning to the office.

Another reason why it's harder to build a sense of belonging in hybrid work is 'proximity bias'. Research has revealed that we look more favourably on those people we see more often. Connecticut-based Synchrony Financial has told its leadership team that they cannot return to the office five days a week. Instead, they are required to work at least one day from home. DJ Casto, chief human resources officer at Synchrony Financial, says that one of the main reasons they adopted this rule was to put home-working and office-working staff on a more equal playing field. 'From a leadership perspective, we want to make sure we look like we're supporting both groups', he explains, noting that 85% of employees in a company-wide survey expressed a desire to work from home full time.[2] Some workers may feel pressured to come back into the office to get more face time with their managers (and thus more recognition, career advancement opportunities, stretch assignments, and glamour work.). Companies like Synchrony are not alone; the awareness of the proximity bias, which is the unconscious tendency to give preferential treatment to people in our immediate proximity, is pushing more employers to create rules and policies to prevent or limit this bias. Proximity bias, like any other type of bias, is a natural human inclination. If we look at our network of friends, most of us have friends who look like us, most likely from the same gender, same ethnic background, same educational background, same age group, same family background, etc. At the same time, this natural inclination can lead to unfair treatment of remote workers and hybrid workers who spend less time in the office with their managers. A Stanford research study revealed that remote workers at a large Chinese travel agency lost out to in-house staff on performance-based promotions, despite delivering higher levels of performance.[3] Proximity bias is very real and can have a negative impact on remote workers' and hybrid workers' sense of belonging in the workplace.

Belonging Boosts Performance, Engagement, and Well-being

According to the McKinsey 2021 Survey, CEOs' top priorities include sustainability, transforming in the cloud, cultivating talent, pressing the need for speed, and operating with purpose.[4] Surprisingly, building belonging was not listed as a top CEO priority, despite all the evidence supporting the business case for belonging in the workplace. According to a 2019 EY survey, more than 40% of workers feel physically and emotionally isolated in the workplace.[5] People require more connection with those they work with. The need for connection and significance is amongst the top human needs (along with certainty, uncertainty, growth, and contribution). If people do not feel a sense of connection and/or significance at work, it will negatively impact how they show up in the workplace. If CEOs want to grow their business, one of the first areas to look at and prioritize is to build a strong culture of belonging and inclusion. A 2019 survey by BetterUp found that high belonging is linked to a 56% increase in job performance, a 50% drop in turnover risk, and a 75% reduction in sick days. For a 10 000-person company, this would result in annual savings of more than $52 million.[6] The study also revealed that employees with higher workplace belonging showed a 167% increase in their employer promoter score (their willingness to recommend their company to others). They also received double the raises and 18 times more promotions. Another finding by the same survey was that, unsurprisingly, feeling excluded *causes* us to give less effort to the team. The study was a series of experiments, in which workers were assigned to a team with two other 'participants' (bots programmed to act like teammates), using a collaborative virtual ball-toss game. *Included* workers had teammates that consistently threw them the ball, whereas *excluded* workers only got the ball a couple of times. After this, participants completed a simple task where they could earn money either for themselves or for their entire team. The longer participants persisted in the task, the more money they earned. What differences manifested between the excluded and included teammates? When participants were told the payouts would be shared with the team, the excluded people worked less hard than the included ones, even though it meant sacrificing earnings. When participants were told the payouts would benefit them and them alone, excluded team members worked just as much as included ones. This exercise was replicated again and again, across four separate studies.

If we want to look at this from a different perspective, let's look at what social isolation does to our health. The US Surgeon General recently stated that loneliness is a more serious health problem than opiates.[7] Many studies link

Employers who prioritize building a culture of belonging in remote work and hybrid work environments will reap the benefits by developing a workforce that is more connected, more engaged at work, healthier, and more productive and collaborative.

social isolation with negative health consequences including depression, poor sleep quality, poor cardiovascular function, and lower immunity.[8] Remote work can lead to feelings of isolation and depression, which eventually impacts the business as well. Employees who feel excluded have lower immune systems and are more likely to take sick days; they are also more likely to have difficulties concentrating at work, which leads to weak decision-making and poor collaboration and communication with their colleagues.

Simply put, creating a sense of belonging at work is good for business.

Fostering Belonging Is Key in Hybrid Work

Hybrid work has fundamentally transformed how we belong and how we connect at work. As human beings, we are hardwired for human connection – at work, informal interactions and bonding constitute what makes the work fulfilling and meaningful. Small talk in the office, meeting at the office coffee station, chatting before and after meetings, or for a happy hour are key parts of the connection process with colleagues.

Now that hybrid work and remote work have become the norm for many and that the opportunities for spontaneous interactions are rare, feelings of loneliness, isolation, and disconnection are more prevalent. Lonely and isolated employees are more likely to get sick, more likely to leave the organization, and more likely to be less engaged and productive. The remedy for loneliness and isolation is camaraderie and connection at work, whether employees are remote or in the office.

To replicate the spontaneous in-person social glue we organically had in the office, employers must proactively build a connected workplace by using all the technologies, strategies, and resources that make it possible. Team leaders, managers, and senior leadership teams must be trained on how to deliberately create, through their daily actions, workplaces that help their people connect with each other, develop bonds, share knowledge, and feel connected and celebrated.

Belonging and connection fulfils one of the human needs, and it translates into better talent engagement, retention, collaboration, and productivity. Human connection also improves our well-being, our physical health, and our mental health. Social connection is so important that neuroscientists even describe it as what makes human beings the most successful species on earth: 'To the extent that we can characterize evolution as designing our modern brains, this is what our brains were wired for: reaching out to and interacting with others', writes neuroscientist Matthew Lieberman in his book *Social: Why Our Brains Are Wired to Connect.* 'These social adaptations are central to making us the most successful species on earth.'[9]

The real competitive advantage at work is where company culture, employee connections, and employees' connection with the company's mission coexist. Creating a common mission that's supported by strong employee connection and appreciation significantly improves talent attraction and retention. Connected, fulfilled employees with a clear mission are more productive, more collaborative, and happier human beings. One way to foster connection, even in a hybrid work environment, is when leaders embrace empathy and vulnerability by talking about their challenges and doubts. This can help others open up and feel psychologically safe to speak up, helping everyone realize that they are having common experiences, ultimately strengthening the relationship between bosses and employees.

Hybrid work environments are a great opportunity for employers to rethink their employer brand and their employee value proposition (EVP). A 2021 McKinsey HR research study revealed that during the Covid-19 pandemic, 39% of employees struggled to maintain a strong connection with colleagues as informal social networks weakened and people leaned in heavily to the people and groups with whom they most identified.[10] That is another reason why employers should invest in figuring out how hybrid social networks work best, along with other ways to help employees establish high-quality relationships, strengthen connections, and nurture trust.

A 2021 Gartner research study revealed that organizations must reinvent their employee value proposition to deliver a more human deal. The research found that providing employees with a more holistic experience increases employee satisfaction with the EVP by 15%. 'Traditionally, organizations focus on employees as workers when they define their EVP,' said Carolina Valencia, vice president in the Gartner HR practice. 'Instead, employers need to see their employees as people first and foremost. Our research shows that 82% of employees say it's important for their organization to see them as a person, not just an employee, yet only 45% of employees believe their organization actually sees them this way.'[11]

Overall, employers should focus on one objective: in the new hybrid work world, they will need to prioritize proactive measures and actions for creating connection and a sense of belonging. It's now a business imperative.

Endnotes

1. https://www.newswire.ca/news-releases/remote-work-creating-barriers-to-inclusion-and-belonging-as-pandemic-continues-855363453.html

2. https://www.bbc.com/worklife/article/20210804-hybrid-work-how-proximity-bias-can-lead-to-favouritism

3. https://www.gsb.stanford.edu/faculty-research/publications/does-working-home-work-evidence-chinese-experiment

4. https://www.mckinsey.com/business-functions/strategy-and-corporate-finance/our-insights/what-matters-most-five-priorities-for-ceos-in-the-next-normal

5. https://hbr.org/2019/02/the-surprising-power-of-simply-asking-coworkers-how-theyre-doing

6. https://hbr.org/2019/12/the-value-of-belonging-at-work

7. https://www.hrmonline.com.au/employee-engagement/belonging-hr-leadership/

8. https://www.healthassured.org/blog/isolation-and-mental-health/

9. https://greatergood.berkeley.edu/topic/social_connection/definition

10. https://www.mckinsey.com/business-functions/people-and-organizational-performance/our-insights/its-time-for-leaders-to-get-real-about-hybrid

11. https://www.gartner.com/en/newsroom/press-releases/2020-05-25-gartner-hr-research-shows-organizations-must-reinvent-their-employment-value-proposition-to-deliver-a-more-human-deal

3 The Four-Pillar Framework

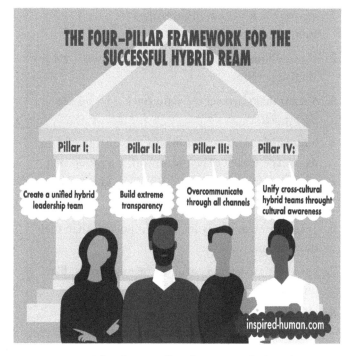

Figure 3.1 The four-pillar framework for the successful hybrid team.

What makes a team really successful in hybrid work? There is a lot of information and advice on the Internet about what makes a team successful, and not all advice has been created equally. In fact, there are many myths and misconceptions about what makes a team really successful; I think it is important that we immediately identify bad advice so that we can start with a fresh perspective. Here are some of the most damaging myths about teamwork that can be found on the web:

1. Team members must choose or compromise between getting the job done and treating one another humanely.

2. Teambuilding means taking time away from 'real work' at offsite events.

3. A team that starts on the right track stays on the right track.

4. Individuals aren't responsible for the quality of their team experience because teamwork is a group skill.

5. Managers and consultants are responsible for building teams.

6. Team members' skills are more important than their motivation.

7. For a team to be successful, its members must like one another.

8. Harmony helps. Smooth interaction among collaborators avoids time-wasting debates about how best to proceed.

9. Face-to-face interaction is passé. Now that we have powerful electronic technologies for communication

and coordination, teams can do their work much more efficiently at a distance.

10. You need many tools to have efficient teamwork in hybrid work.

11. All you need is a group of people with the right skills.

All these myths about teamwork are extremely damaging because they are based on incorrect assumptions. In today's workplace, team managers, business leaders, entrepreneurs, and those who manage people need the right tools and strategies to build an extraordinary team that will achieve incredible results in a hybrid work environment. Today, more than ever before, as the world is adjusting to a post-pandemic reality, the time has come for leaders to learn the right strategies to lead a successful team in a distributed environment. In every country and in every continent, organizations of all sizes need to become aware of the strategies to use to develop world-class teams in a remote working environment. Remote work and hybrid work are here to stay and remote teams and hybrid teams are becoming the new standard. In this new hybrid work setting, teams must learn how to become exceptional despite the geographical distance between coworkers. Having successful hybrid teams will make or break an organization; its greatest asset is its people, and if its people are not working well together in this new hybrid environment, it's a fast-track to failure. By using a proven framework, leaders can develop world-class teams in a hybrid-work environment to build a truly successful organization that not only survives, but also thrives. One team leader who worked for an organization I consulted for – a mid-size technology company headquartered in San Francisco with offices in Europe and Asia-Pacific – shared with me one thing she really loved about remote work. She said that when her company had to rapidly move from office work to remote work in April 2020, one of the things she noticed was how her colleagues became more 'real'. Meetings were now happening from people's homes; she could see her teammates' kitchen tables and kids in the background, and her co-workers opened up about more personal stories for the first time. For instance, one of her team members, a mum of two young children, shared that she was struggling to work from home with the kids around; that then led to more authentic conversations between them. Remote work and hybrid work environments can be fantastic in developing stronger and more authentic bonds and connections between colleagues when it is done the right way.

In this book, I want to share the four-pillar framework that I have used to help thousands of people create successful teams in hybrid work. Creating world-class teams that are engaged, productive, collaborative, and innovative is the most important strategy for a business, and even more so now, in a world that will be increasingly hybrid with people working from different locations and working together on projects.

Over my many years of consulting for organizations of all sizes in regard to their workplace culture, I have observed a pattern that makes teams successful. In particular, in a hybrid work setting, where employees are geographically distributed, I have noticed first-hand what strategy the most successful teams are using over and over again to achieve great collaboration and improved performance. I call it the four-pillar framework because it is a simple strategy that is anchored around four key elements. The first pillar is about creating a unified hybrid leadership team; the second pillar is about building extreme clarity and transparency; the third pillar is about overcommunicating through all channels; and the fourth pillar is about unifying cross-cultural remote teams through cultural awareness. Each pillar will share strategies and techniques that you can use to develop a truly world-class team in your organization in a hybrid work setting. Each pillar will also contain some stories and anecdotes to illustrate how these techniques have been implemented successfully in other organizations. The four-pillar framework has been built with a specific order in mind:

The first pillar focuses on getting the fundamentals right: creating a unified hybrid leadership team. This is a key, fundamental stepping stone to your strategy and should be done first – and should be done right – before you move on to the next step.

The second pillar involves building extreme clarity and transparency and can only be achieved once you have created a unified hybrid leadership team. Your job – to build extreme clarity and transparency – isn't easy but is absolutely fundamental if you truly want to develop a world-class team in hybrid work.

The third pillar relates to intentional overcommunication through all the channels available. This step is a key element of the four-pillar framework and can sometimes be overlooked by leaders who assume this is an easy step; in reality, it takes conscious, daily effort to be an excellent communicator, especially in a remote work or hybrid work environment.

Finally, once these three strategies have been implemented, you can start to unify your team – the fourth pillar – through cultural awareness. This final step is equally critical because it allows all your people to understand each other and build empathy and connections in the long term, which will ultimately improve team collaboration, boost team communication, and set the foundation for creative thinking and innovation through psychological safety. It is critical that every step is implemented in the right order and with care if you want to develop a world-class team in a hybrid work environment.

This framework has been tested and proven across hundreds of teams, thousands of people, and many organizations of different sizes and across different industries. I have tested this framework with high-tech companies, food manufacturing companies, engineering firms, and aviation companies, and all these companies achieved better performance once they implemented this framework in their teams. I have shared this framework with start-ups that have just 50 employees, small and medium-sized companies with a few thousand employees, and large enterprise organizations with 45 000 employees, and again, each organization achieved better performance once they implemented this four-pillar framework. I have also helped organizations use this framework with teams based in the United Kingdom, North America, Europe, and Asia, and every organization obtained better results after implementing this framework. It is my sincere hope that you will also find business success and achieve improved performance once you implement this four-pillar framework in your own team and across your own organization.

4 Pillar I: Create a Unified Hybrid Leadership Team

PILLAR I – CREATE A UNIFIED HYBRID LEADERSHIP TEAM

- Use values to unify
- Role-modelling and setting the tone
- Setting common goals
- Create opportunities to co-lead
- Schedule informal time

inspired-human.com

Figure 4.1 Pillar I – Create a unified hybrid leadership team.

Introduction

When a family is unified, it doesn't matter what business they're in. They can successfully transition from one generation to the next.

Andrew Keyt

Although leadership teams are not family, if they are unified, they will be successful in managing world-class teams. A few years ago, a San Francisco–based software company asked me to help them fix a problem they were having regarding what they called a toxic workplace culture. The CEO complained that his leadership team were not getting along, and they were constantly arguing over how to operate the business. As a result, the business growth had been slowing down, the company was struggling to hit its revenue goals, and deadlines were often missed. When I joined the first meeting with the senior leadership team, I immediately spotted a few patterns. The chief marketing officer's (CMO) approach to business was completely separate from and even clashing against the chief revenue officer's (CRO) approach to business. Each of them had different goals, each of them strongly believing that their own set of goals was the one and only, and each of them not listening to the other party. What's more, both of them seemed more aligned with their subordinates than with their peers; this translated into fruitless leadership meetings, poor business performance, and a very toxic work environment where blaming was common practice. As I started working with the group and sharing some of the strategies and techniques to build a high-performing and inclusive team, I noticed a shift in the way the CMO and CRO treated each other. One morning in particular, as we were going through one of the workshops, I caught the CMO saying to the CRO, 'I realize that I have not taken your goals into consideration as much as I should have, and I want to change that. I have been revisiting my marketing strategy and including your goals, and I asked my team to also be measured on new goals that include yours'. This was an 'aha' moment for the entire leadership team and a real turning point. From that moment onwards, the entire culture of the leadership team shifted from a blame culture to a unified team culture, and it translated into every aspect of the business. Within a few months, the business's revenue was getting back on track and its growth accelerated.

In this chapter, I will share the strategies and techniques that you can use in order to create a unified hybrid leadership team. I will share the steps that you can take in order to build unity amongst your leadership team when some members work from the office, some work from home, and some work in geographically dispersed locations. Many business leaders have asked me over the last 18 months how they can continue to lead hybrid teams successfully, even after the Covid-19 pandemic. How can they balance trust, engagement, and unity in this new complex way of working? As a diversity and inclusion consultant and author who spent a decade studying what makes teams successful, I spent years working with teams and, in particular, with hybrid teams to identify what makes them successful in a hybrid environment. I would like to share some well-known leadership myths that should be avoided at all costs:

1. Leaders have all the answers

This is a very damaging claim. On the contrary, leaders have a very clear understanding of their own limitations, which helps them build unity with their peers. Leaders know that constant growth and learning is what makes a great leader. They also understand that leading is a team sport, and they must seek help from their peers if they want to be successful. 'If you want to go fast, go alone; but if you want to go far, go together', says the African proverb. Great leaders understand that unity with their peers through asking questions is key to great leadership.

2. Great leaders are born, not made

The idea that leadership is an inherited feature rather than a skill that is learnt is very dangerous and damaging; the skills that make a leader great are learnt and developed, like any other skill. I would actually argue that a great leader is entirely made and not born; all the skills that make a leader great are human skills that anyone can develop: communication, accountability, empathy, humility, resilience, vision, influence, confidence, and positivity. Great leaders constantly grow by learning from their peers, which creates great unity in the group.

3. Leaders must eliminate mistakes

On the contrary, leaders see mistakes as an opportunity to learn and grow. Great leaders can see the difference between work that is lacking and unforeseen mistakes. Unforeseen mistakes demonstrate that the employee is taking risks and being accountable for their work, which leads to growth; unified leadership teams make mistakes together and grow together.

In summary, great leaders know that unity in leadership is key, and they rise above the most common leadership misconceptions; they understand what it takes to create a truly unified leadership team in hybrid work. Outstanding leaders attract, develop, and retain successful teams in a hybrid world by building unity amongst their leaders, especially in hybrid work.

Using Values to Unify

> As your leadership team is the glue that keeps your company together, your first job as a leader is to build unity in your leadership team.

The most efficient way to achieve unity in your leadership team is to use your company values to unify them. In a crisis like the Covid-19 pandemic, or in any other crisis for that matter, the main goal is to navigate through it. Take the time to ensure that your company values are consistent with where you want your organization to be headed. When you use your company values to communicate to your leadership team how to move forward, you are communicating to them your DNA and your company culture, inviting your leadership team to embody your company values themselves. In a hybrid environment, the importance of your company values as the glue that keeps your leadership team together is more important than ever before. When the Covid-19 pandemic started impacting businesses in March 2020, many organizations contacted me to request help with building successful teams and resilient company cultures during these challenging times. One organization in particular was struggling with the crisis; it was a UK-based scale-up with 500 employees, and they had grown so fast that they didn't have a strong, unified leadership team at the top. When the Covid-19 pandemic hit, they noticed they were losing employees faster than they could hire new ones. Their employee retention rate had always been a challenge but, since the pandemic, they were losing employees at such a rapid rate that it was beginning to impact their bottom line. The company was suddenly unable to rely on their old ways of operating. When I started working with the leadership team, I asked the group what their mission statement was. A big silence followed. None of the senior leaders was able to come up with the company mission statement. We did an exercise whereby I asked each team member to write down answers to the following questions: What do we do? How do we do it? Whom do we do it for? What problem do we solve? What solution do we offer? After they had written all their answers, I asked each team member to share them with the group. What followed was a passionate discussion about the company values. The team really came together for the first time and were able to articulate the company values as a unit. They took this opportunity to revisit the mission statement and shared the company values with their entire team.

From that day forward, the leadership team used the company values as a compass to make all the important decisions related to the business. In that instance, we did this exercise virtually over Zoom because of the restrictions at the time related to Covid-19. However, I highly recommend that this exercise is done face-to-face wherever possible because it brings an element of greater connection and bonding. Once the unifying values of the company are in place and understood by the leadership team, it becomes easier for the management team to partner successfully with their employees to solve the company's challenges in a hybrid work environment. In a fully remote environment, I strongly recommend that you start each meeting with a reading of the company values to help everyone understand them and be driven by these values. One of the great benefits of unifying your leadership team through values is that it empowers them and all the people in your company to take charge. Think about it this way: when each employee is clear about the company values, they are empowered to make decisions because they know what values are important in this organization. This, in itself, improves employee engagement and removes bottlenecks and micromanagement. In hybrid work in particular, providing a value framework is critical because hybrid work itself creates additional challenges. Hybrid work can be used as an opportunity to revisit your company culture and values.

A June 2020 survey from the *Insurance Journal* revealed that isolation from co-workers was among the biggest challenges that workers were experiencing in remote work.[1] Feelings of isolation are increased if the team is newly remote. In remote or hybrid work environments, social interactions are much more limited than in traditional office environments.

Keeping your company values alive in a hybrid environment requires work but is completely worth the investment. There are many techniques that you can use to keep your values alive in hybrid work to unify your leadership team, and these include:

1. Hosting virtual lunches and breakfasts for your leadership team with a focus on values and culture.

2. Creating a value Slack channel for your leadership team to encourage more discussions on that topic.

3. Hosting regular virtual value workshops for your leadership team.

4. Sending weekly or monthly pulse surveys to your leadership team asking how they feel on company values.

5. Communicating often via different channels on the topics of value and culture.

Implementing these techniques will help you build and nurture unity within your leadership team in a remote or hybrid work environment; more importantly, it will help your management team rally around your core values, which is fundamental to building a successful team in hybrid work.

A great example of a company using values to unify their leadership team is Salesforce. The famous customer relationship management (CRM) platform was built in 1999, when the four Salesforce founders launched the system from a small San Francisco apartment. All the software and customer data would be hosted on the internet and be available as a subscription service. This was groundbreaking at the time, and was the beginning of what we know today as 'software as a service', or SaaS. One element that was key to the success of this team of four was their unity around their values; the small team knew that they needed to cultivate trust with their customers in order to convince them to use this innovative technology. By cultivating unity through the shared value of trust, the team was able to grow the unknown start-up to the $21- billion annual revenue software giant we know today. As Salesforce themselves write on their website when talking about the company story: 'Early adopters of our cloud-based model took a significant leap of faith. There was only one formula for earning their trust – that is, by building trusted relationships.'[2] Salesforce values are unique as they are almost entirely focused on their employees and customer base, and they include:

- Trust
- Customer success
- Innovation
- Equality

Salesforce even has a chief equality officer as part of the leadership team, as a concrete embodiment of their values and as a symbol of how important the company values are to unify the leadership team.

Unifying the leadership team around core values can be a challenging task, especially if you have not done this exercise before. So it's important to take a minute to explain what we mean by company values, why they are important, and how to identify them. *Harvard Business Review* defines core values as the deeply ingrained principles that guide all of a company's actions. Collins and Porras define core values as being inherent and sacrosanct; they can never be compromised, either for convenience or short-term economic gain.[3] For all employees to work towards a shared mission and goal, it makes sense that the company has its

Company values should be visible in every part of the business as they are a key pillar of the company culture. A great exercise to unify your leadership team is to help them identify your company core values themselves.

own set of core values. Company values are here to guide actions, behaviours, and decisions.

If your company already has core values, you will still benefit from refreshing them and from unifying your management team around your company values. The following is a guide to help your leadership team identify or revisit your company values to ultimately become more unified:

1. **Articulate who is involved in the process**

    Be clear about who is leading the process of identifying the company values. Ideally, your entire leadership team should be involved because this will create unity and alignment. Make it clear that all leadership team members are equal in making the decision. Ensure that everyone gets a chance to speak and moderate the meeting. If your group is larger than five people, you might use the round-robin method to ensure equal share of voice. You might even appoint a meeting moderator to allow equal opportunity to contribute.

2. **Get commitment and buy-in**

    Without the full buy-in from your leadership team, you won't get the alignment and unity you need within your management team. Ask your leadership team members what values are important to them individually and how their contributions to the company values could help them achieve their aspirations. If any leader doesn't seem be on board, you might speak to them individually. Try to understand their motivations and use them to get buy-in to the project. Take the time to ensure that each and every one of your leaders is committed to identifying and/or revisiting your company values so that they will become fully unified around your company values during this exercise.

3. Encourage research

A great way to get your leadership team to identify or revisit your company values is to encourage them to look around. Invite your management team to get inspired by finding companies with inspiring core values. Ask your leaders to write down what values resonate with them most, what makes these values relevant to them, and how these values could become your company values moving forward. By getting your leaders to actively research and write down values, you are getting them emotionally involved with the work and more engaged with your company value project.

4. Consolidate

Ask your management team to share the company values they have identified. Invite your leadership team to combine all these values into one final set of core values. Encourage your leaders to integrate the best values and the ones that resonate most with your organization. Invite your leadership team to articulate what they mean in your organization.

Using company values to unify your leadership team is key to creating a successful team, and especially in hybrid work, where employees are hungry for connection through shared values.

A great example of a company using its core values to unify its leadership team is Xerox. In 2001, when former CEO Anne Mulcahy was appointed CEO, the organization was $18 billion in debt, and on the verge of bankruptcy. The company had recorded losses in each of the preceding six years. Customers were unhappy, and to top it all, Xerox found itself in the middle of an investigation by the Securities and Exchange Commission concerning accounting improprieties in its Mexico unit. According to a 2008 US News article, Mulcahy met personally with the top 100 executives.[4] She let them know how dire the situation was and asked them if they were prepared to commit. A full 98 of the 100 executives decided to stay, and the bulk of them are still with the company today. Mulcahy reported that she always felt great pride in staying true to the company values, rather than capitulating to Wall Street and the bankers. Anne Mulcahy was a champion of Xerox and its core values; as someone who had worked at Xerox for 24 years when she was appointed to the role of CEO, she believed in the loyalty of customers and especially employees and executives. Her leadership team understood what was at stake and became unified and aligned around the company values. 'We wouldn't have survived if we didn't have that love and loyalty,' she told US News. Another great example of a company that used its core values to unify the leadership team in a crisis is Chobani. In 2013, Chobani's yogurt cups started exploding (literally) in the supermarkets where they were being sold.[5] A batch of products had been contaminated by bacteria causing a pressure inside the yogurt cups, leading to explosions. The leadership team quickly came together and made a few decisions based on the company core values: first, they immediately recalled the yogurt cups made in its Idaho plant, then, they jumped on social media to apologize and to personally address every tweet about the incident. According to *Wired*, the brand replied to over 3600 tweets in only 5 days.[6] AdAge reported that CEO Hamdi Ulukaya shared his plan to write a personal letter to each of the 150 000 people that had an issue with its product because he takes it very personally and very seriously, and he wanted to thank them for sticking with him and standing by him.[7] By making decisions based on the company values, the CEO and its leadership team were able to create a unified response to a crisis. To this day, the company values of Chobani remain strong and include:

- Giving back
- Innovation
- People

The company's mission statement consolidates these values as follows: 'Chobani is a food maker with a mission of making high-quality and nutritious food accessible to more people, while elevating our communities and making the world a healthier place.' Using values is the first step to creating a unified hybrid leadership team. Like Xerox and Chobani, you can leverage your organization's core values as the glue to align your leadership team.

Role Modelling and Setting the Tone

On a cold day in January 1961, Fred Schultz, a truck driver, slipped and fell on an icy sidewalk and broke his ankle while working. Fred ended up stuck at home with his foot up for more than a month. When Fred didn't work, he didn't get paid. Fred's wife was seven months' pregnant, so she couldn't work either. Fred's son, Howard, was seven years old when the accident happened. At the dinner table, Howard and his sister ate silently while their parents argued about how much money they would have to borrow. Sometimes, the phone would ring in the evening and Howard's mother insisted he answer it: it was a bill collector and Howard was instructed to say his parents weren't at home. 'That image of my father, slumped on the family couch, his leg in a cast, unable to work or earn money and ground down by the world, is still burned in my mind,' the Starbucks CEO once said. Young Howard Schultz vowed that if he was ever in a position where he could make a difference, he wouldn't leave people behind. The story serves as the foundation for how the Starbucks CEO's behaviour became an example and inspired many to follow his good behaviour. Schultz's values manifested in nearly every initiative Starbucks implemented during his time as CEO: health benefits for part-time workers, tuition assistance, veterans hiring, and an employee stock purchase programme. 'Starbucks has become a living legacy of my dad,' Schultz said.

A role model, like Howard Schultz, is someone other people look up to in order to help determine appropriate behaviours. Positive role models offer a range of helpful or useful behaviours. Visibility plays an important part in making someone a role model. Leaders are the most visible members of their organizations, making them more likely to become role models for the rest of the employees. Since many employees can observe their leaders' behaviour, it is likely and natural that many of them will imitate their attitudes. Younger employees, in particular, are more likely to emulate a leader's behaviour because they are still developing their own identities.

If your leadership doesn't set the tone, they will not share a common standard, and each leader will follow their own standard. This will lead to a mismatch, and issues will arise in projects involving cross-collaboration. If your managers don't model a good attitude, they will be more likely not to trust each other, creating disconnection between teams, building a toxic environment, and diminishing collaboration and communication. According to a 2020 survey by The Workforce Institute, more than half (58%) of employees say a lack of trust affects their career choices, including nearly a quarter (24%) who left a company because they didn't feel trusted.[8] The study also found that poor trust even hurts talent pools: one in five employees (22%) actively didn't refer a friend, family member, or former colleague to an open role because they didn't trust their company. Negative role models instil a lack of trust; in its 2016 global CEO survey, PwC reported that 55% of CEOs think that a lack of trust is a threat to their organization's growth.[9]

> Asking your leadership team to become role models is a great way to create a unified leadership team, especially in hybrid work. If your leadership team fails to model good behaviour in hybrid work, they will set the tone for less-than-good behaviour being considered acceptable in your organization.

Modelling good behaviour in hybrid work or remote work can be a challenge. Many business leaders naturally wonder how they can effectively set the tone when their teams are working remotely, and they are not as visible to all their team members. There are effective ways to model good behaviour and set the tone in hybrid work environments. In particular, there are four ways that leaders can become inspiring role models for their teams in hybrid work:

1. Building trust

This might seem counterintuitive at first, but being intentionally silent instead of solving all the issues can be more effective in building trust because it allows team members to feel valued. Great leaders refrain from rushing to fix things; instead, they invite their team members to find solutions by themselves.

> A great way to build trust is to refrain from rushing to fix things but instead, allowing team members to think through challenges themselves and to come up with their own solutions.

Another powerful strategy to build trust is to say when you do not know. Employees have been conditioned to feel that they will be punished if they do not know all the answers at work. However, nobody has all the answers all the time, so this assumption is simply untrue. You need to change the expectation that people should know everything in your team. Creating the tone that it is OK to not know everything is a great way to change that false assumption. For example, you can celebrate when someone says they don't know. Encourage your team to explore different perspectives for each scenario, showing them that more than one option is always possible, and by doing so, you are demonstrating that it is OK not to know everything, but rather it is better to be open to new ideas and perspectives. Think of how to ask questions that allow people to say they don't know.

Allowing team members to think through challenges themselves and saying when you don't know can be done remotely; leaders can refrain from rushing to fix things and change the expectation that people should know everything even in a distributed environment.

2. Adopting a positive attitude

Presenting a positive attitude at work seems obvious and straightforward; however, it takes conscious effort and intentional actions to achieve a consistently positive attitude at work.

Being mindful about how much time is spent with negative co-workers can help keep a positive attitude. Being careful not to take part in negative talks, gossip, or drama will also help maintain a positive mindset.

> When the entire leadership team commits to adopting a positive attitude together, no matter what, they automatically surround themselves with positive people: their peers.

Being mindful of what information is being consumed is another great way to nurture a positive mindset. Listening to positive music, uplifting audiobooks, and following positive people can make all the difference. Choosing positive language and becoming more conscious of the words being used helps nurture a good attitude. For example, when an unexpected situation arises at work that significantly disrupts the course of the business, choosing to say, 'This is an interesting challenge that will make us identify new and better ways to operate,' would be more positive than saying, 'This is a crisis that will have negative impacts on the business in profound and very disruptive ways.' Being nice to colleagues is another great way to nurture and develop a positive attitude at work. When being nice to colleagues becomes a regular occurrence, a cycle of generosity and kindness is created, making the instigator feel good as well as the recipients of the act of kindness. In this way, the positive attitude spreads in the organization. Being mindful, meditating and breathing exercises, as well as regular physical exercise all create the right environment to cultivate a positive attitude. Encouraging your leadership team to keep and nurture a positive attitude will help them model good behaviour and become a unified leadership team, which is especially important in a hybrid work environment.

3. Inspiring their team

Setting a clear goal to inspire their team is a great way to invite your leadership team to model good behaviour in remote work. Inviting your managers to foster a growth mindset with their teams will help them become role models themselves. Offering personal and professional development opportunities, encouraging continuous learning (online or face-to-face), normalizing feedback, and encouraging knowledge sharing via Slack channels are great ways that your management team can inspire their own teams, even in a hybrid work environment. Focusing feedback on the effort of the team rather than the outcome is a powerful way to foster a growth mindset to inspire people. Feedback sessions should be focused on the steps that employees took in order to achieve a goal. Inviting your leaders to proactively ask their team for regular feedback is a great way to foster a growth mindset and ultimately to inspire; this can be done in hybrid work by using a Slack channel for feedback, or by starting or ending your online meetings with, 'What can I do better right now?' With a regular feedback loop that is normalized, employees will naturally strive for continuous improvement.

When people adopt a growth mindset and a culture of feedback by mirroring their leaders, they feel like they are in the driver's seat of their careers, which makes them fully engaged at work. In a hybrid work setting, this can be easily achieved through regular pulse surveys that can be completed online.

> The more leaders inspire through a growth mindset, the more people will be inspired and embrace a feedback culture.

4. Exhibiting integrity

Establishing a culture of integrity in your leadership team means that each leader shares a sense of mutual trust and accountability. Integrity can be defined as aligning one's conduct with what they know to be excellent. Leaders with integrity always seek to reflect ethical standards and do the right thing regardless of whether someone is watching or not. When your leadership team acts with integrity, it gives everyone peace of mind in knowing they will do the right thing regardless of the outcome. First and foremost, you must convey the importance of integrity within your leadership team. A great way to do that is to simply ask your management team the following questions, and let them come up with their own answers:

◆ What makes integrity important in our organization?

◆ How will integrity allow them to do their best work?

◆ Who do they need to work with to exhibit high levels of integrity?

When you help your leadership team understand the value of integrity, they will become more likely to exhibit high levels of integrity themselves and model that positive behaviour with their respective teams. Invite your team to repeat this exercise by asking employees questions about integrity in team meetings. Your leaders can host a virtual meeting with their individual teams and discuss the power and value of integrity and what makes it important to a team's success. Encourage your managers to find creative ways to embed integrity in their own teams. In a hybrid work environment, modelling integrity will be a key element of a team's success since there is less visibility and employees are not monitored as closely.

In their best-selling book *The Leadership Challenge: How to Make Extraordinary Things Happen in Organizations*, authors James M. Kouzes and Barry Z. Posner wrote, 'Exemplary leaders know that if they want to gain commitment and achieve the highest standards, they must be models of the behaviour they expect of others.' The authors also said, 'When leaders are doing their best, they model the way, inspire a shared vision, challenge the process, enable others to act, and encourage the heart.'[10] Georgetown University's McDonough School of Business Professor Christine Porath, who studies civility in the workplace, found that bad behaviours are contagious.[11] In her famous *Harvard Business Review* article, she reveals that even the simple exposure to rude words can affect employees' abilities to process information and perform up to standard. Porath recommends that leaders start by examining the way they interact with others. She calls attention to this surprising fact: 'Verbalizing negative thoughts is 10 times more damaging to our sense of well-being than if we simply think about them.'[12] When leaders verbalize negative thoughts among their peers or team members, they negatively impact their peers' well-being as well. Another study by the *Work and Stress* journal found that leaders who showed up to work while feeling ill had workers who were more likely to do the same. That study highlights the fact that leaders must not only say what the expectations are but also model the expectations themselves.[13] In other words, leaders failing to model good behaviour themselves also fail to build teams that act as they are expected to. If your leaders say they expect employees to act with integrity and respect, but they are unreliable, lie, and criticize colleagues in front of others, then the whole team is likely to be unreliable, lie, and criticize colleagues in front of others.

As research demonstrates, great leaders who act as role models and who set the tone for what behaviour is acceptable are more likely to build teams that act as role models themselves, which creates a more unified leadership team.

In hybrid work, there are many ways that leaders can exhibit positive behaviour to unify their teams around the same values: allowing team members to think through challenges themselves and to come up with their own solutions, which can be done via emails and Zoom calls; creating a Slack channel called 'shoutouts' to praise a great attitude; sending regular pulse surveys to teams to collect feedback, and host virtual meetings to discuss feedback and actions to improve; hosting virtual meetings to discuss the power of integrity and brainstorm ideas to embed integrity in the team. Like Howard Schultz, you can become the role model that unifies your leadership team by setting the tone and exhibiting integrity and positive behaviour.

Setting Common Goals

When Leanne Beesley joined Giggster early in 2021 as the general manager for Europe, it was her first experience managing people. She recalls, 'As I started scaling the team and scaling the company, honestly, I felt a bit overwhelmed. I wasn't from a business background.'[14] One day, Beesley came across Andrew Grove's *High Output Management* book, and discovered Objective and Key Results (OKRs) as a tool to accelerate collective output. 'As soon as I worked with the team to implement OKRs, our growth just skyrocketed,' she says. Within a year, their revenue increased by 2628%. Before the company used OKRs, she said that it sometimes felt like each team was building 'separate houses'. They all had their individual quarterly plans that weren't always necessarily connected to a cohesive vision. OKRs allowed the teams to create plans that moved them forward toward a common goal, says Beesley. 'So we created a really strong foundation for success by laying the bricks together to build one epic mansion.'

OKRs are an effective goal-setting leadership tool for communicating what a team wants to achieve. OKRs can be extremely helpful in aiding a leadership team set common goals. Common goals give a group of people a shared purpose. They encourage people to work together as a unified team and to achieve an end result. Common goals are strategic in nature, and they are a company's objectives that the leadership establishes to outline expected outcomes and to guide their employees' work. Establishing common goals directs employees' efforts, justifies a company's activity, sets standards, and helps eliminate unnecessary activity. Common goals inform the entire team about the company's destination and its plan to get there. Common goals can also be referred to as shared goals, common objectives, and common purpose.

In their book *The Strategy-Focused Organization*, authors Robert Kaplan and David Norton reported that 'a mere 7 % of employees today fully understand their company's business strategies and what's expected of them in order to help achieve company goals'.[15] A 2015 Gallup study revealed that half of employees strongly indicate that they know what's expected of them at work.[16] Gallup reviewed data from 550 organizations and 2.2 million employees, and they also found that the managers of these employees are equally unclear on what is expected of them. Gallup also found that only 12% of employees strongly agree that their manager helps them set work priorities, and just 13% strongly agree that their manager helps them set performance goals. Gallup highlights that highly engaged employees want ongoing feedback, and they want to be held accountable.

When the leadership team takes the time to set common goals, the benefits to the business are countless. Setting common goals within the leadership team helps boost engagement and productivity because it helps leaders understand what their role is within the leadership team. Shared goals also help save time and improve efficiency, as it avoids having leaders pursuing different objectives. When leaders share common goals, it creates transparency because communication is open and each team member knows what everyone else is working on. Everyone in the team knows exactly what the team is working on, since the common goal has been made clear. When the leadership team shares a set of common goals, it also means that every leader understands the wider purpose of what they are doing, which creates motivation. Common goals create a sense of purpose, they connect team members to the organizational purpose, which fuels their work. When leaders share common goals, it means that one leader's success is everyone's success. Leaders are then more likely to actively help each other and work collaboratively in the pursuit of the same goals; common goals within the leadership team fosters better collaboration and reduces competition within the team.

In a hybrid work environment, where employees are more disconnected from each other, ensuring that leaders share common goals is even more important to the success of the organization. Although it can be difficult to unify the leadership team in a remote or hybrid work environment, it is critical to do so, and it can be done by following specific steps:

1. **Identify business goals**

    The first step for setting common goals for your leadership team is to identify the business goals. As the business owner, chairperson, CEO, or leader, your role is to facilitate the process and let your leaders contribute so that they feel emotionally involved. Remember that your primary goal is to create a unified leadership team in hybrid work, so helping your managers identify and clarify the business goals is key to uniting your leaders. This exercise is better done in person because people can be more present in the discussion when physically in the same room. However, if it is not possible to gather your leadership team in the same room, this can be done in a virtual meeting. If done virtually, ensure that you brief your team members about the importance of this exercise and you expect their full attention during the virtual meeting; do not tolerate distractions such as phone calls or meeting interruptions. If you have some leaders in the room and some leaders attending remotely, tell your in-person leaders to minimize private conversations during this exercise, as this can distract the remote leaders and make them feel excluded. Setting the tone for what behaviour is expected during this exercise will be a key factor to the success of setting common goals.

As the leader, your role is to facilitate and guide the conversation rather than answering questions yourself; having said that, you can certainly offer guidance and ensure that the business goals that are identified by your leadership team are aligned with yours. Ensuring that you let your leadership team come up with their own answers about what the business goals are is a key part of this exercise, because it creates accountability and ownership within your team members; identifying business goals will keep your leadership team aligned towards a shared objective. Some questions you might ask your leaders to help them with setting business goals include:

1. What does our company stand for? What are our values?

2. What is the reason the company was created?

3. Where do we want the company to be in 10 years, 20 years and 30 years?

4. What is one goal that will never be compromised for other goals? In other words, what value is more important than any other value in our company?

2. Set SMART team goals

Once you have helped your leadership team identify your business goals, you must then move onto the next step of setting common goals: setting SMART team goals. A SMART goal is a tool that helps plan and achieve a goal more effectively. The SMART acronym stands for Specific, Measurable, Achievable, Realistic and Timely. When your leadership team sets SMART team goals, they are much more likely to focus their efforts and to achieve their goal. Specific SMART team goals have significantly higher chances of being achieved.

> As you facilitate this exercise with your leadership team, remember that identifying your business goals requires clarity. Ensure that your leadership team is crystal clear about your business goals and that they are fully committed to these goals as well.

Here are some questions you should ask your leaders when doing this exercise:

1. Are our team goals specific enough?
2. Are our team goals measurable? If so, how will we measure our goals?
3. Are our team goals achievable?
4. Are our team goals realistic?
5. Do our team goals have a timeline associated with them?

This exercise of setting SMART team goals is better done face-to-face for maximum participation; however, if face-to-face is not an option, it can be done in a hybrid work setting, provided that all leaders are fully engaged in this session, avoiding conflicting meetings and distractions such as Slack notifications or phone calls, etc. If this exercise is done in a hybrid work setting, in which some leaders are in the same room and some leaders are joining remotely, it is critical that the meeting host allocates equal speaking time for each participant; you might appoint a meeting host to moderate speaking time. Here are some examples of SMART team goals:

- Achieve 90% customer satisfaction across all geographies within the next 6 months.
- Launch new product within the next 6 months and achieve new product adoption with 30% of our client base in the next 9 months.

– Secure 500 paid registrants to our Summit in
6 months, and achieve $750 000 in opportunities
from Summit within 3 months after Summit.

Make sure that your SMART team goals are aligned
with the business goals that have been previously
identified by your team.

3. **Document team goals**

A study by psychology professor Gail Matthews at
the Dominican University in California revealed that
people are 42% more likely to achieve their goals if
they write them down.[17] As Pablo Picasso famously
wrote: 'Our goals can only be reached through a vehicle
of a plan, in which we must fervently believe, and upon
which we must vigorously act. There is no other route
to success.' Documenting goals in writing increases the
likelihood of achieving them and keeps everyone
accountable. Ask each of your leaders to write down
the team goals in their strategy and have them share
their strategy with each other, including yourself. Here
are some recommendations you might share with your
leadership team as they document the team goals:

1. Use active words, such as 'we will increase our
customer NPS to 90% within the next 6 months
across all geographies.'

2. Articulate how each leader will play a role for each
goal. Don't have just one leader or a few leaders be
solely accountable for a team goal– every leader
should play an active role for each team goal.

3. Be specific and clear about what success looks like.

4. Connect each team goal to the business goals and the
organization's values.

In a hybrid work environment, documenting team goals is more important than ever because people are more isolated than before; writing down team goals and sharing them is key to create a unified team in hybrid work or remote work.

4. **Measure progress through check-ins**

A 2016 Censuswide survey revealed that 50% of companies that tracked metrics in real time met all their goals in the last 12 months compared to only 24% of companies that didn't track in real time.[18] The study also found that 92% of companies that tracked their metrics in real time met some or all their goals in the last 12 months compared to 64% of companies that didn't track in real time. When we measure progress often, we are more likely to achieve our goals. Many teams forget to set regular check-ins to track progress, which leads to a lack of progress overall. Once you have identified your business goals, set SMART team goals, and documented team goals, you must set up regular team check-ins to track progress. Ideally, this should be done at the same time as you identify business goals, set SMART team goals and document team goals, so that the complete exercise is done, and no step gets forgotten. Simply invite your leadership team to create a cadence meeting and to add 'tracking progress' as part of the agenda. In a hybrid work environment, this cadence meeting can be virtual and doesn't need to be face-to-face; however it's important that each member of the leadership team shares an update regarding the team goal tracking during each meeting. The key is to avoid having only a few leaders sharing updates regarding certain team goals in these cadence meetings because this would send the message that only they have

responsibility for certain team goals. You might even
add the name of each leader next to the 'measuring
team goal' agenda item, to set the expectation that each
leader will have to share an update on progress against
each team goal.

Setting common goals for your leaders is critical to
creating a unified leadership team, especially in a hybrid
work or remote work environment. The importance of a
unified team that is aligned is highlighted by the story of the
Google Aristotle project. In 2012, Google launched Project
Aristotle. Google analysed data about employees on more
than 100 teams at the company.[19] The study found that in
the best teams, members show sensitivity, and most
importantly, listen to one another. Google's study
highlighted that the best teams are mindful that all members
contribute to the conversation equally. When a team is
unified, it has the right foundation for being successful.
Creating a unified leadership team in hybrid work can be
challenging, but it can be done by following the steps
highlighted above. When you build a unified leadership
team, you set the foundation for a successful team. Setting
common goals is a key factor in achieving unity within
your team.

Creating Opportunities to Co-Lead

In 1895, Lord Kelvin, a world-renowned mathematical
physicist, stated that 'heavier-than-air flying machines are
impossible'.[20] That same year, Thomas Edison himself
stated: 'It is apparent to me that the possibilities of the
aeroplane, which two or three years ago were thought to

hold the solution to the [flying machine] problem, have been exhausted, and that we must turn elsewhere.'[21] Even Wilbur Wright said in 1901 to his brother Orville that 'man would not fly for 50 years.'[22] However, on December 17, 1903, the Wright brothers made their first flights with their first powered aircraft. What allowed the Wright brothers to succeed against all the odds? How did the two brothers create what seemed to be impossible at the time, when other, better-funded entrepreneurs were failing at inventing the modern aircraft? Although the answer is probably a combination of multiple elements, co-leadership is a key factor for the success of the Wright brothers. Wilbur and Orville understood the power of leading together. According to their mechanic Charlie Taylor, Wilbur and Orville were never really mad at each other. One morning after one of their 'hottest' exchanges, he had only just opened the shop, when Orville came in saying he 'guessed he'd been wrong and they ought to do it Will's way.' Shortly after, Wilbur arrived to announce he had been thinking it over and 'perhaps Orv was right.' The point was, said Charlie, 'when they were through. . .they knew where they were and could go ahead with the job.'[23]

Co-leadership is having two or more leaders sharing equally the responsibilities for a team, a project, or an objective. The American Psychological Association defined co-leadership as 'the sharing of the organizational, directive, and motivational duties of leadership between two or more individuals.'[24] According to a 2002 study by Pearce and Sims, shared leadership is a useful predictor of team effectiveness.[25] When we analyse what makes co-leadership so successful, we can easily identify three main reasons. First, co-leadership improves buy-in from different teams.

Co-leaders are forced to challenge each other's perspectives all the time, engaging in productive conversations that lead to a more measured decision based on multiple perspectives.

Co-leaders represent their own team, department, and geography and therefore their people feel represented at the top. Second, co-leaders make better decisions.

Third, co-leaders set the tone for a culture of collaboration. When employees see leaders always working together as a team, they see a behaviour of collaboration and are more likely to emulate that collaborative behaviour themselves.

Creating opportunities for leaders and managers to co-lead is an extremely powerful way to create a unified leadership team. Particularly in a hybrid work environment, where employees are naturally more isolated and disconnected from one another, cultivating ways for leaders to lead together creates bonds and strengthens the relationships. Here are a few ways you can create opportunities for co-leadership:

1. Match leaders intentionally

When thinking about matching leaders for a co-leadership project, it's important to think about your outcome. What are you hoping to achieve with this co-leadership team? What result do you wish to get with this specific team of leaders? How will this co-leadership further unify your leadership team? If some of your leaders are not as aligned or as unified as you want them to be, consider asking them to become a unit by inviting them to co-lead a specific project together. This might be exactly what they need to come together. It might feel counterintuitive to match leaders who are not as aligned as you want them to be; however, co-leading a project is an effective way to make people collaborate and find ways to make things work no matter what. Equally, consider matching leaders from departments that do not usually interact; for example, you might match your chief marketing officer with your chief technical officer, or your chief human resources officer with your VP of engineering; these cross-functional co-leadership teams will spark some creativity and innovation, opening up new collaborations that will further align your leadership team.

2. **Monitor and facilitate the relationship between co-leaders**

Co-leadership projects will inevitably bring some conflicts between the two leaders. It is important to remember that not all conflict is bad. Healthy conflict is actually essential for the success of the organization because it allows everyone to feel heard and valued, and it helps reach the best outcome for the business. Expect conflict. Tell your leaders to anticipate natural, healthy conflict during their co-leadership journey, and normalize healthy, productive conflict within your leadership team. Communicate to your leaders that healthy conflict is good and is a sign of people pushing through their limits and focusing on the best possible outcome for the business. Encourage your co-leaders to establish some rules that will help them reflect on their co-leadership dynamics: scheduling a weekly meeting to discuss what is working, what needs improvement, what should be stopped, what should be done differently.

Remind your co-leaders to ask for help when they
meet a roadblock and check on the co-leadership
projects often.

3. **Remind co-leaders to define roles and responsibilities**
    As with any relationship, communication is key
and especially when communicating what's expected of
the other person. Remind your co-leaders that they
should discuss their roles and responsibilities in this
co-leadership project, and they should come to their
own conclusion by themselves. The key here is that
co-leaders have an open discussion about what each
expects from the other, so that everyone is clear about
their role and their responsibilities; this process should
be a continuous discussion that takes place often, as
things will evolve, and therefore, their roles and
responsibilities will evolve too. Encourage your
co-leaders to be open and honest about who owns
what and to keep each other accountable; remind your
leaders that co-leading can feel challenging at times,
but it is all part of the process of creating more
alignment in your leadership team, and if everyone
focuses on that alignment outcome, the process will be
more enjoyable.

4. **Bring the fun into it**
    Wait. . .did we just say 'fun' in a business book?
Absolutely! Leaders are human beings, and they are
moved by emotions. Don't let the pressure and stress of
being a leader get in the way of what makes every
human want to share time with others: having fun!
Without creating any 'forced fun', you can instil a sense
of humour and fun in your co-leadership projects.
Co-leaders who are having the most fun in their

projects are often those who also are the most successful with their projects. Find ways to have fun at work yourself and your leaders will model it; when you see your leaders having fun, communicate to them that it's a great thing! Create fun by finding ways to make co-leading a fun activity; A BrightHR study found that 62% of employees who took no sick days in the previous three months had fun at work; and 58% of those who took 11-plus sick days reported not having fun at work.[26] Having fun at work makes people feel more engaged and ultimately more collaborative. Remind your leadership team that fun is important, and share fun moments often with your wider team to increase engagement and collaboration.

Leading during a crisis such as the Covid-19 pandemic and managing the needs of remote employees can take its toll on managers. An increasing number of CEOs and business leaders have been sharing their struggles with burnout and stress. This has led to a wider adoption of the co-leadership model, with more co-CEOs sharing the responsibility than ever before.

Roleshare co-CEOs Sophie Smallwood and Dave Smallwood say that being co-CEOs of the company was 'a way of alleviating some of the mental burden of being CEO'. Sophie and Dave explain that being co-leaders of the company provides 'an extra layer of confidentiality and vulnerability that not even your closest C-suite ally can offer – regardless of whether you're married.' Sophie Smallwood added that it can be lonely to be at the top of the organization because of the demands from many people. Co-CEO Sophie Smallwood also confessed that it is hard to be positive all the time, and if you are alone it can make it even harder. 'In a partnership, you can lift each other up,' says Sophie Smallwood. The co-leadership model clearly worked out well for Sophie and Dave Smallwood, who went from just 2 to 12 employees in only 4 years and have already attracted sought-after investors including Techstars[27].

UK media company Jungle Creations also adopted the co-CEO model as a way to accelerate growth. Jungle Creations co-CEOs believe that it takes more than one leader to be prepared for what lies ahead. Jungle's co-CEO Nat Poulter shared that having another leader to 'stress-test new ideas against' leads to better outcomes; Jungle's co-CEO Melissa Chapman believes 'it makes for more effective, hands-on leadership.' Clearly the move from a single CEO model to a co-CEO model paid off for Jungle, whose employee count increased from just 132 in December 2020 when the co-CEO model started, to 153 employees (and counting!) in December 2021.[28]

Although the co-CEO model is still relatively rare and not widely reported in the media, many successful companies are embracing this co-leadership model. Netflix has had two CEOs since 2020, with co-founder and long-term CEO Reed Hastings responsible for the streaming side of the business and Ted Sarandos focusing on Netflix's content. American online retailer of prescription glasses Warby Parker has embraced the co-CEOs model since day one: co-founders and co-CEOs Dave Gilboa and Neil Blumenthal have shared the realm since 2010, when they founded the company. The two co-founders went to college together and decided to start a company to offer prescription glasses at an affordable price, providing a great user experience. The success of the company has been so big that

Warby Parker received a $3 billion valuation when it raised $245 million in August 2020.[29]

A study published by Wiley in 2011 named 'It Takes Two: The Incidence and Effectiveness of Co-CEOs' found that 'co-CEOs generally complement each other in terms of educational background or executive responsibilities'.[30] Even more encouraging, the study revealed that 'the market reacts positively to appointments of co-CEOs, while a propensity score analysis shows that the presence of co-CEOs increases firm valuation.'

Thomas Asseo, co-CEO of the US's largest organic ready-to-eat meal delivery service, Fresh n' Lean, explains that the co-CEO model helped take his company to the next level; Asseo reveals that his company achieved $87 million in revenue in 2020, which is more than double from the previous year. Asseo believes that the co-leadership model allows him and his co-CEO Laureen Asseo (his sister) to complement each other. During the decade that Thomas and Laureen served as co-CEOs, their company Fresh n' Lean grew from a very small team to 475 employees, they delivered 17 million meals, partnered with key brands in the sports and fitness industry, and grew their revenue exponentially. Laureen Asseo adds, 'There was too much for one person to oversee as a CEO and not enough hours in the day.'

One of the main benefits of the co-leadership model is that it creates alignment at the top and it unifies the leadership of an organization. Co-leaders share more than just a project or a team, they share a relationship, a partnership. Working together every day creates a special sense of belonging, a special purpose. The proximity created by co-leadership facilitates better decision-making; another lateral effect of leading together is the better access to information that would not be otherwise possible. The constant discussions simply provide more opportunities to bring up different pieces of information that would otherwise not be shared. Each leader gains a better understanding of what is happening in the other leader's department or business units, which leads to more informed decisions. Co-leadership also brings balance to decisions. Having another perspective added to the single, narrow perspective of just one leader, often leads to more balanced decision-making and a better outcome for the business. The knowledge, experience, expertize, and approach of one leader will always add value to the other leader's perspective. Co-leaders often complement each other through their skill sets, their way of thinking, their network, and their life experiences. Although decisions might take a little longer, the benefit of co-leadership outweighs that because the decisions are more often than not better, more balanced, and lead to better business outcomes.

Co-leadership in hybrid work can happen just as easily, if not better, than in an office setting; by leveraging Slack, Zoom, and Google Drive, remotely leading a project or team together can happen just as effectively.

Having regular meetings between the two leaders remains an essential element of making the co-leadership model work. Any opportunity for the co-leaders to strengthen their relationship will help make their work better; if possible, it is helpful to arrange regular face-to-face, informal reunions such as face-to-face breakfasts, lunches, or dinners, to build a strong relationship that's not just built remotely over Zoom.

Schedule Informal Time

When Jennie Kim got engaged, she decided to get in shape for
her wedding. Unfortunately, her job at Udacity meant that she
was spending more time snacking than exercising. So when she
found out that her co-worker was also getting married and
wanted to get in shape too, she decided to play Dance Central
once a week in her company's game room. 'I find that these
sessions help re-energize me for the rest of the day,' said Jennie
Kim.[31] Jennie's informal time at work is not an isolated case. At
Udacity, creating informal occasions to bring people together
for a fun event is part of the company culture. Udacity hosts
'Fancy Fridays': these are days when people can dress up to fit a
theme. Past themes included Bumpit Friday (big hair), Fancy
Feet, Oscar Night, and Panda (everyone wore black and
white). Udacity also hosts regular 'Recess' after work; these
events are usually a small party focused on something fun such
as making snow cones, dim sum, or ice cream.

Employees of 91Springboard started chasing the ball as
a team-building exercise, but today they are taking part in
full-blown football matches early in the morning, before
work.[32] Anil George, vice president of operations at
91Springboard, says, 'While "work, work" may not be
discussed at all during these games, spending time with
those you don't get a chance to meet during work hours
helps people approach each other with a sense of comfort
that eases work.' Ayush Pranav, a 25-year-old portfolio
analyst at 91Springboard, also agrees that these football
games helped him get access to colleagues he would not have
otherwise had access to: 'The matches are fun, but the other
upside is that we get to mingle with the senior management.
That works out well for all of us.'

An informal situation is one which is relaxed, friendly, and not very serious or official, according to *Collins Dictionary*.[33] Informal gatherings at work are events that are less planned and regulated than formal meetings. Team building, in particular, can be defined as the process of turning a group of people into a more cohesive team. Team building refers to different types of activities aimed at improving social relationships; both informal meetings at work and team-building activities help improve the alignment of a group of people and strengthen a team.

Team-building activities and informal gatherings at work are extremely powerful ways to create a unified leadership team, which is especially important in a hybrid work environment.

When Sandy Pentland, professor at MIT Management Sloan School led a research study on teams who consistently deliver higher performances, he found an interesting pattern. Pentland equipped teams (comprising 2500 individuals from a variety of projects and industries) with wearable electronic sensors to collect data on their social behaviour.[34] The data revealed that the most important predictor of a team's success was its communication patterns. The researchers could foretell

> Non-formal meetings significantly improve communication because people open up more in a relaxed atmosphere. Informal meetings also increase productivity as a result of better communication and collaboration, they improve morale and motivation, they encourage creativity, they build more trust and respect and add more fun to the world of work.

which teams would outperform just by looking at the data on their communication. Pentland identified three key communication dynamics that affect performance: energy, engagement, and exploration. The research found that team members who have side conversations within the team, who take breaks together, and who catch up on non-work topics frequently were part of the most successful teams.

Another similar study published in the MIT Sloan Management Review found that hybrid teams can outperform teams working in an office together if collaboration is managed properly.[35] The study researched the performance of 80 different teams with different levels of dispersion. The research found that key drivers of performance are processes that facilitate communication among members. The study revealed that 'social processes that increase team cohesion, identification, and informal communication help establish and maintain interpersonal bonds that enable a group to better cope with conflicts'. Those social processes helped improve the performance of remote and face-to-face teams. The research clearly indicates that informal time that creates stronger connections is a strong predictor of a team's performance.

When organizations facilitate informal meetings and team-building activities, they create a more unified team that performs better. But in a highly distributed team, how can you facilitate informal time to achieve better connections? There are different ways that you can schedule informal time in a virtual or hybrid environment.

Set Up Non-Work-Related Spaces

When associate professor of human resource management at Rutgers School of Management and Labor Relations, Jessica

Methot, studied small talk at work, she found something remarkable. Methot studied 150 employees and observed their daily actions at work in pre-pandemic times.[36] Methot found that on days participants had more small talk, they felt higher positive emotions including friendly feelings, gratitude, pride, and more energy. What's more, that positive emotion based on small talk improved participants' well-being and gave them more energy to help their colleagues. Methot argues that small talk builds trust and rapport.

In a hybrid work setting or a remote work environment, organizations that create spaces for such small talk are able to better build rapport, trust, and positive feelings among their workforces. Slack is a great tool to create spaces for employees to talk about non-work-related topics and to replicate the water cooler chats from the office. You can create Slack channels that are dedicated to non-work topics, including pets, family, games, motivation, travel, etc. One of the most popular topics on Slack channels is 'furry friends'. Employees love sharing pictures and videos of their favourite pets. Animal lovers get to share photos of their beloved pets on the dedicated Slack channel, and this gets the conversation started between people from different teams and departments very easily.

Employers could set up similar non-work-related Slack channels just for the members of their leadership team. By creating a dedicated Slack channel called 'weekend plans' for your leadership team, you will encourage small talk and informal conversations between your leaders, even if they all live in different places. The more your distributed leaders share personal stories and anecdotes about their weekends on that Slack channel, the more they will build rapport and trust and lift the levels of energy within the group. This will create rapport and cohesion, which is something to seek in a hybrid work model. Think of Slack like a virtual water cooler. An even better way to encourage all leaders and all employees to be active in these non-work Slack channels is to encourage the CEO to be an active participant. When the CEO leads by example and shares personal stories and anecdotes in the 'furry friends' and the 'weekend plans' Slack channels, other leaders and employees will mirror their CEO's behaviour and share their own personal stories too. Research has shown that even a simple email sent from the CEO to all employees, stating the importance of something, such as sharing personal stories and talking about non-work-related topics, can largely influence the adoption of a behaviour. In summary, set up non-work-related Slack channels for all employees and also for your leadership team, take an active role in using these channels, encourage your leaders and employees to actively use the channels, and share the message that small talk is important.

Host Virtual Breakfasts, Lunches, and Coffee Breaks

When Randi Lippert moved to London, she was looking forward to meeting her new colleagues. However, her move took place during the first Covid-19 lockdown, meaning that she never really got a chance to bond with her new colleagues. Randi still got a chance to meet with her new colleagues, thanks to her employer's Zoom lunches. Her employer, Wealthsimple, pays for lunchbox deliveries to staff at their home address and invites everyone to eat while socializing virtually. Randi shares that joining her company's virtual lunches once a week has helped her during a challenging time. 'Remote lunches have been an amazing way to have dedicated time and space to socialize with my

colleagues', says Randi, 'it has truly cultivated a sense of
camaraderie and support during what has been an extremely
weird and often isolating time.' When business psychologist
Stuart Duff was asked about virtual lunches, he confirmed
that having video lunches with colleagues can be very
beneficial for employees working remotely because remote
workers miss having opportunities for fun and spontaneous
conversations with their colleagues.[37] There are many
different ways you can host a virtual breakfast, lunch, or
coffee break and there is certainly no one-size-fits-all;
however, there are certain specific elements that you might
consider before hosting yours.

Pick a day and time that suits most people

This
might sound obvious, but often, people are not able to join
due to conflicting schedules. You might send out a survey,
asking your team which day and time best suits them and
send your virtual event invite accordingly. Even better, you
want to consider making this event repeatable each week, so
that you demonstrate that virtual get-togethers are
important in your organization. Take into consideration
time zones if your team is dispersed across many different
countries. You might even decide to rotate the time to make
it fair for everyone in your dispersed team.

Pay for your team lunches

Paying for your team
lunches is important because it demonstrates that it is your
organization that wants to facilitate social interactions
between all colleagues. It also sends the message that your
organization values time spent together socializing. Decide
on a budget per person, and share easy instructions to your

guests on how to order and expense their virtual team lunch. Make it easy for your team to order and expense their virtual lunches as this should be something your team looks forward to, rather than something they dread.

Test the format   Try different formats and let your participants get involved. Some virtual lunches can be very casual with no agenda; some might start with icebreakers, whereby each participant gets to share an answer to a question. You can use icebreaker question generators found on the internet. As the CEO or team leader, make sure that you participate in these team lunches because this will send the message that they are important. Don't be afraid to share some personal stories and anecdotes because this will show others that they can do the same, and this will create a deeper connection between all team members.

Virtual lunches, breakfasts, and coffee breaks are easy to implement and can be a lot of fun. As hybrid teams have few opportunities to connect in an informal setting, virtual get-togethers offer a chance to connect and create meaningful relationships that in turn create a more unified team.

Host Group Learning Sessions

LinkedIn's 2018 Workplace Learning & Development Report found that 94% of employees would stay at a company longer if it invested in their career development.[38] Another study by Udemy titled the '2016 Udemy Workplace Boredom Study' revealed that 80% of employees surveyed agreed that learning new skills would make them more engaged at work.[39] Learning and development sessions at work boost employee engagement, improving collaboration in the workplace.

Collaborative learning, in particular, is when employees who share their experiences and knowledge increase their knowledge and connect on a deeper level.

Collaborative learning involves participation, socialization, conversation, and reflection.

Also called group learning or team learning, it refers to people in groups learning from each other. Researchers Marjan Laal and Seyed Moha studied the benefits of collaborative learning in their 2012 research.[40] The researchers found that one of the main benefits of collaboration learning is the social benefits; they found that it helps develop a social support system for learners, it builds diversity understanding among staff, it establishes a positive atmosphere for modelling and practising cooperation, and it develops learning communities.

CEOs and team leaders should consider hosting group learning sessions, especially within their leadership team, to align their team through increased collaboration. Group learning sessions can be facilitated online to support teams working in a hybrid work environment. A great way to facilitate group learning sessions is to invite each leader to host their own group learning session based on a topic of their choice. This allows each leader to share their experience in a specific domain and allows the rest of the group to learn collaboratively by asking questions.

Scheduling informal time is a powerful way to create a unified leadership team in a hybrid work environment.

Whether this is done by setting up non-work-related spaces such as a Slack channel on pets, family, or weekend plans; by hosting weekly virtual lunches that are facilitated by the company; or by hosting group learning sessions, facilitating time for the team to socialize in a distributed environment will create a more unified and aligned leadership team.

Conclusion

When a workforce is made up of teams working from home, teams working in the office, and team members distributed across the world, many challenges arise that can hinder the growth of the organization. Employees working in isolation from each other can feel more disconnected and disengaged from their peers and from their work, and this can hinder collaboration, communication, customer service, customer support, and user experience because disengaged employees will deliver lower performances which, in turn, will be felt by their peers, customers, and by the market. Distributed teams have more difficulties communicating in real time, which leads to slower decision-making and more mistakes. Employees working remotely may also feel less part of the team or less supported in their choice of work compared to their office-working colleagues.

However, the hybrid work model is here to stay, and companies must find ways to create highly successful teams that thrive in a hybrid work model. One of the main components of a successful hybrid team is a highly unified and aligned leadership team. A study by LSA Global found that highly aligned companies grow revenue 58% faster and are 72% more profitable while significantly outperforming their unaligned peers.[41] Employees need their leaders to remind them often of their organization's mission, yet 33% of employees don't feel like they are reminded of their company's mission often enough.[42] In a study by Clear Company, 97% of employees and executives believe lack of alignment within a team impacts the outcome of a task or project, and 86% of employees and executives cite lack of collaboration or ineffective communication for workplace failures.[43] Alignment is key to organizational success, and it is the leadership team who drives alignment from the top. Particularly in a distributed environment, creating a highly unified leadership team is key to the success of the organization.

As a CEO or team leader, there are different ways that you can create a unified leadership team in a distributed work environment. Building alignment and unity within your leadership team takes time and commitment, but it can be achieved, even in a distributed organization. Values are a powerful vehicle of human behaviour, and leveraging common values to unify your leadership team should be considered if you want to create a unified team. Host virtual lunches for your leadership team with a focus on values and culture, and create a value Slack channel to encourage discussions on that topic. Facilitate regular virtual value workshops, sending weekly or monthly pulse surveys asking how your team feel about company values and communicating often via different channels on the topics of value and culture. Help your leadership team identify your company core values by themselves to develop even more commitment to your company values. If your company already has core values, you can still benefit from refreshing your core values and from unifying your management team around them. The second step to creating a unified hybrid leadership team is role-modelling and setting the tone. Role models are individuals other people look up to in order to help determine appropriate behaviours. Positive role models offer a range of helpful or useful behaviours. Visibility plays an important part in making someone a role model. Asking your leadership team to become role models is a great way to create a unified leadership team, especially in hybrid work. Encourage your team to build trust by refraining from rushing to fix things but instead allowing their team members to think through challenges themselves and to come up with their own solutions. Invite your leaders to present a positive attitude at work, because even though it might seem obvious, it takes conscious effort and intentional actions to achieve a consistent positive attitude. Invite your people to set a clear goal to inspire their team: it is a great way to invite your leadership team to model good behaviour in remote work. Encourage your managers to foster a growth mindset with their own teams because it will help them become role models themselves; establish a culture of integrity in your leadership team whereby each leader shares a sense of mutual trust and accountability. Integrity can be defined as aligning one's conduct with what they know to be excellent. Leaders with integrity always seek to reflect ethical standards and do the right thing regardless of whether someone is watching or not.

Remember to set common goals for your leadership team. When the leadership team sets common goals, everyone understands what their role is within the team. Shared goals help save time and improve efficiency because it avoids having leaders pursuing different objectives. It also creates transparency because communication is open and focused. Most importantly, when a team shares common goals, it means that one team member's success is everyone's

success, so leaders are more likely to actively help
each other.

The fourth element of creating a unified leadership
team is to create opportunities to co-lead. Co-leadership
improves buy-in from different departments because each
co-leader represents their own department, and their people
feel represented at the top. Co-leaders make better decisions
because they are forced to challenge each other's perspectives
all the time. Co-leaders also set the tone for a culture of
collaboration because when all employees see leaders
working together collaboratively, they see a behaviour of
collaboration and are more likely to emulate that
collaborative behaviour themselves. Creating opportunities
for leaders to co-lead is an extremely powerful way to create
a unified leadership team.

Finally, the fifth element of creating a unified
leadership team in a hybrid work setting is to schedule
some informal time for the people to create stronger
relationships. Non-formal meetings at work significantly
improve communication because people open up more in a
relaxed atmosphere. Informal gatherings also increase
productivity as a result of better communication and
collaboration; they improve morale and motivation,
encourage creativity, build more trust and respect, and add
more fun to the world of work. Setting up non-work-
related spaces such as informal Slack channels can help
create a more unified leadership team in hybrid work;
hosting virtual breakfasts, lunches, and coffee breaks that
are facilitated and promoted by the CEO can create spaces
for the team to come together. Hosting group learning
sessions can also strengthen bonds between a team because

they encourage collaborative learning and discussion in a less formal setting.

Creating a unified hybrid leadership team is a critical strategy to build a successful hybrid team because creating alignment and unity at the top allows everyone to navigate in the same direction, regardless of where they work. However, simply creating a unified hybrid leadership team is not enough, and some work must be done to further set your organization up for success. Building extreme clarity and transparency is another critical strategy to achieve success in hybrid work.

Endnotes

1. https://www.bizjournals.com/portland/ news/2020/08/21/how-to-use-core-values-to-unify- your-company-in-a-crisis.html

2. https://www.salesforce.com/company/our-story/

3. https://hbr.org/2002/07/ make-your-values-mean-something

4. https://www.usnews.com/news/best-leaders/ articles/2008/11/19/americas-best- leaders-anne-mulcahy-xerox-ceo

5. https://www.foodsafetynews.com/2013/09/ chobani-pulls-yogurt-cups-says-no-recall/

6. https://www.workhuman.com/resources/ globoforce-blog/5-companies-whose-great-cultures- saved-their-bacon

7. https://adage.com/article/news/ recall-chobani-touts-quality-campaign/244940

8. https://www.businesswire.com/news/
home/20201215005273/en/Trust-is-the-
Foundational-Imperative-of-2021-Global-Research-
by-The-Workforce-Institute-at-UKG-Explores-Why-
Trust-is-Hard-to-Find-at-Work

9. https://hbr.org/2017/01/the-neuroscience-of-
trust#:~:text=Leaders%20understand%20the%20
stakes%E2%80%94at,t%20sure%20where%20to%20
start.

10. https://www.goodreads.com/work/quotes/1756095-
the-leadership-challenge

11. https://www.youtube.com/watch?v=py4P8b4t3DI

12. https://hbr.org/2020/10/how-to-thrive-when-
everything-feels-terrible

13. https://www.tandfonline.com/doi/abs/10.1080/02678
373.2020.1728420?journalCode=twst20

14. https://www.whatmatters.com/articles/
how-giggster-is-using-okrs-to-scale-their-business/

15. https://inside.6q.io/setting-team-goals/

16. https://www.gallup.com/workplace/236567/obsolete-
annual-reviews-gallup-advice.aspx

17. https://www.inc.com/peter-economy/this-is-way-you-
need-to-write-down-your-goals-for-faster-
success.html

18. https://www.geckoboard.com/blog/
us-smbs-who-set-and-track-key-metrics-are-2x-
more-likely-to-hit-targets-survey/

19. https://www.scoro.com/blog/
teamwork-stories-importance-of-teamwork/

20. https://www.newscientist.com/article/
dn13556-10-impossibilities-conquered-by-science/

21. https://www.xaprb.com/blog/flight-is-impossible/

22. https://www.thoughtco.com/famous-quotes-
of-the-wright-brothers-1992679

23. https://academyleadership.com/news/201610.asp

24. https://dictionary.apa.org/coleadership

25. https://www.researchgate.net/publication/298971419_
Vertical_versus_shared_leadership_as_predictors_of_
the_effectiveness_of_change_management_teams_
An_examination_of_aversive_directive_transactional_
transformational_and_empowering_leader_
behaviors

26. https://peopledevelopmentmagazine.com/2017/04/14/
fun-workplace-productive

27. https://www.crunchbase.com/organization/roleshare/
company_financials

28. https://digiday.com/media/more-businesses-are-
trying-co-ceo-leadership-models-to-help-offset-
exec-burnout/

29. https://www.barrons.com/articles/
warby-parker-direct-listing-51632867371?tesla=y

30. https://onlinelibrary.wiley.com/doi/
abs/10.1111/j.1540-6288.2011.00305.x

31. https://wavelength.asana.com/
workstyle-6-companies-get-teamwork-right/#close

32. https://www.livemint.com/news/business-of-life/
informal-meetings-are-key-to-innovative-
ideas-1553022288691.html

33. https://www.collinsdictionary.com/dictionary/
english/informal

34. https://hbr.org/2012/04/
the-new-science-of-building-great-teams

35. https://sloanreview.mit.edu/article/
how-to-manage-virtual-teams/

36. https://www.nasdaq.com/articles/the-understated-
importance-of-office-small-talk-2021-02-26

37. https://www.bbc.co.uk/news/business-55716899

38. https://learning.linkedin.com/content/dam/me/
learning/en-us/pdfs/linkedin-learning-workplace-
learning-report-2018.pdf

39. https://info.udemy.com/rs/273-CKQ-053/
images/2016_Udemy_Workplace_Boredom_Study.pdf

40. https://www.sciencedirect.com/science/article/pii/
S1877042811030205#!

41. https://lsaglobal.com/insights/proprietary-
methodology/lsa-3x-organizational-alignment-model/

42. https://www.minsilo.com/organizational-alignment/
why-is-alignment-important

43. https://technology-signals.com/
the-importance-of-organizational-alignment-and-how-
to-achieve-it/

5 Pillar II: Build Extreme Transparency

Figure 5.1   Pillar II – Build extreme transparency.

Introduction

In November 2013, after several months of internal salary transparency, social media company Buffer took its employee salary information public for the first time.[1] At the time, Buffer's Chief Happiness Officer Carolyn Kopprash admitted she felt scared. 'There were so many unknowns,' said Kopprash. 'We kept going down this rabbit hole of "what ifs".'[2] After the public release of the salaries, Kopprash started seeing the positive impact it created on the organization. 'Our transparent salaries and formula removed the potential for any discrimination' commented Kopprash. 'Your value is your value, no matter your ability to negotiate.' Since releasing their salaries publicly, Buffer received 229% more job applicants. Buffer also saw the quality of their candidates rise after becoming more transparent on their salaries.[3] At the time of writing this book, the company is worth US$60 million and enjoys healthy growth rates. Buffer's CEO Joel Gascoigne shared that the company's employees embraced the transition to salary transparency because they liked having a culture of transparency.[4] As a result, conflicts about compensation are rare. Another benefit of being more transparent about salaries, according to Gascoigne, is that the company now attracts the type of person who is fully onboard with the company's values of transparency.

Buffer didn't stop at increasing salary transparency. Today, anyone can see the company's equity breakdown, revenue, term sheets, diversity numbers, and the code used by its engineers. Internal emails are also shared and the CEO shares with all employees his interactions with investors. Gascoigne commented: 'It really helps with having great teamwork and less politics. Taking the extra step and making it public is extending that trust to customers, blog readers, and prospective team members.'

Transparency in the workplace is the idea of openly sharing information and knowledge in an attempt to benefit the entire business and its employees. From executive leaders openly discussing company information with the entire organization, to individual contributors sharing feedback, to the company discussing company data with members of the public. Transparency affects everyone in the organization, not just the CEO or the C-suite executives. When an organization is transparent about its financial position, employees know whether their job is secure. Similarly, when a business is transparent about its salaries, the right type of job applicants are attracted to the company, and candidates are clear about what they can expect from the company. Transparency in the workplace is about cultivating a culture where information can be shared freely between people, departments, and organizations. Most importantly, workplace transparency is a practice, not just a philosophy. It is about being honest and open about the good things as well as the challenges being faced. A transparent workplace cultivates open communication and collaboration without the element of fear of being judged, blamed, or ridiculed. In a transparent work environment, all employees feel that they are being kept in the loop and are given the full context, so they fully understand what is happening in their organization.

A transparent workplace benefits the organization in many different ways and can truly set the scene for a successful team. Although some benefits of a transparent organization are well known, other advantages are less known but still as impactful. Below are some of the top advantages of a transparent workplace culture:

- **Transparent workplaces facilitate hiring**
  Candidates are attracted to organizations with a transparent workplace culture. In fact, 96% of jobseekers say that it's important to work for a company that embraces transparency, according to a 2017 Glassdoor US Site Survey.[5] According to ExpenseOnDemand, nearly two-thirds (64%) of millennials believe that complete transparency is the most desirable trait from employers.[6] Candidates are simply more attracted to organizations that actively promote and embrace transparency.

- **Workplace transparency boosts employee engagement**
  Transparency at work creates trust and psychological safety, which has often been rated as the top factor of employee satisfaction in many surveys. When the culture of an organization promotes sharing information freely at every level within every department and every team, employees feel more included and in the know and therefore safer. In turn, this promotes openness, trust, belonging, and engagement.

- **Transparency promotes innovation**
  When information is shared frequently and openly at work, every employee is more likely to get to know about new ideas and projects that they would not normally be aware of. Being exposed to more information and ideas promotes creative thinking, especially in an environment where trust is cultivated,

because individuals are more likely to share their ideas about a specific project. When there is a culture of transparency, everyone is more likely to want to share their own contributions to different initiatives, which promotes innovation at every level in the business.

- **Transparency raises brand awareness**

    Businesses with a strong culture of transparency are much more likely to have employees with a strong sense of belonging and engagement with their workplace. Transparent organizations often have strong advocates amongst their employee base, who feel a greater sense of pride and are much more likely to share it through their social media channels. Proud, engaged employees often share personal achievements related to their work and employer on social media, which increases the brand's awareness in an authentic way.

- **Transparency improves communication**

    When information is openly shared often and at every level in the organization, every employee is more aware of the latest developments. Any new project, programme, or initiative is shared with the entire organization, which reduces the risks of working in silo and increases the chance of working collaboratively. Every employee is more likely to share their work more often and with more people because this is what the rest of their team members are doing.

- **Transparency promotes alignment**

    One of the key challenges of running a successful team is creating alignment between all the different departments. Most organizations struggle with creating alignment internally. When the culture of an organization promotes transparency, alignment is much more likely to happen. This is because the constant free flow of information from every department makes it more difficult to miss what another team is working on and reduces the risk of misalignment between teams and departments.

Those are just some of the most important benefits of workplace transparency - there are many other benefits that could be added to the list. Workplace transparency is a key factor of building a successful team, particularly in a hybrid environment. When employees work in different locations, with some working from home, some working from an office and some alternating between both, it is particularly challenging to foster transparency and sharing information effectively. Promoting a transparent work culture in a hybrid work setting becomes more challenging and more important in order to build, develop, and retain a successful team. In the following sections, we will discuss how to build extreme transparency in a hybrid work environment to build a successful team.

Attract and Retain Transparent People

Adam Wright, CEO, co-founded AGI in 1998. He started noticing some patterns when it comes to successfully attracting employees by using a transparent environment. Adam noticed three strategies that worked really well in order to hire the right people to build a transparent team. First, he noticed that when he shared the good things along with the challenges during the hiring process, he significantly increased his chances of retaining the employee who would be more likely to be attracted to the transparent culture in the first place. Second, Adam found that allowing candidates to shadow existing employees helps reduce employee turnover. Offering jobseekers the opportunity to spend time shadowing current employees gives them a chance to see what the job is really like, and either convinces them it is the right fit, or that it is not. Ultimately, this helps the organization attract the right type of employees who share the same company values, and who are more likely to remain long-term employees. Third, Adam realized that resisting the temptation to fill a position quickly helps attract and retain the right candidate. He found that being open and transparent with his team and letting them know to expect some overtime or extra work while hiring the right candidate ensured better communication, and avoided having to start the hiring process all over again if the new recruit left the organization due to a hasty hiring decision.[7]

Attracting and retaining transparent people who share the same core values of your organization is a cornerstone of building a successful team. But transparency is not just expected of the employer, it should also be expected of the candidate. After all, if your organization goes above and beyond to create extreme transparency in the workplace but you hire a candidate who is secretive and doesn't share information openly, not only are they going to damage the culture of your company, but also, they are probably not going to be a good fit for your organization, nor stay in the long term. Below are some strategies that you can use in order to attract transparent people during the hiring process:

- **Check candidates' references rigorously**
  Although the practice of reference checking during the hiring process is well known, there are still many employers who skip that important step in the

hurry to secure a candidate. According to a 2018 HR.
com report by the National Association of Background
Screeners, only 60% of employers conduct background
checks;[8] employment checks are an important part of
background checks, so many employers still fail to
conduct reference checks during the hiring process.
And when employers actually implement reference
checks for their prospective candidates, they often don't
hear good things about them. According to a
CareerBuilder study, three-in-five (62%) of employers
said that when they contacted a reference listed on an
application, the reference didn't have good things to say
about the candidate, and 29% of employers reported
that they have caught a fake reference on a candidate's
application.[9]

When checking a candidate's references,
remember to ask permission first. Ensure that the
candidate approves the reference check. This is a great
opportunity to establish trust with your candidate.
Remember to describe the position to the reference
contact you are calling so that they have as much
context as possible about the role. Ask open questions
and listen without interrupting. Remember to confirm
dates of employment, job titles, responsibilities, and
any achievement that is shared in the candidate's
resume as well as any accomplishments the candidate
shared verbally during the interview process.
Document everything so that you can go back to your
notes if needed at a later stage. Contact the references
yourself if you are the hiring manager, rather than
using a third-party agency, because you are the person
who will be working with the candidate and it's
important that you speak with previous managers to

get as much context and background as possible about your prospective employee. In a hybrid work environment, where your prospective employee might join remotely or in the office, attracting transparent candidates is even more important than in a traditional office setting because the work will be based on trust and reliability. Take the time to check your prospective candidate's references to ensure that they are being as transparent with you as you are being with them.

- **Give candidates an assessment**

   According to the Talent Board's Candidate Experience Research report, 82% of companies are using some form of pre-employment assessment test.[10] Pre-employment assessment tests are a great way for employers to test the candidate's skills, work style, and experience before hiring. Assessment tests are a great opportunity for employers to assess how transparent the candidate is based on the information they shared previously on the resume or during the first interviews. Luckily, there are many different types of pre-employment assessment tests that employers can choose from depending on the role that the organization is hiring for. Assessment tests can include skills assessment tests, measuring a candidate's soft skills and hard skills; they can be job knowledge tests, measuring a candidate's expertize in a specific area; they can be personality tests that are helpful to understand a candidate's way of working and communication style; they can also include cognitive ability tests, measuring problem-solving skills and reasoning. Regardless of the type of assessment test you choose, you should make sure that you use some type of test to assess your

candidate's skills and expertize based on the
information they previously shared with you because
this will allow you to measure how honest and
transparent the candidate has been with you
throughout the hiring process.

- **Research the candidate online**

    Just like your prospective employee will research
    your organization online, you should also research your
    prospective employee online. Online employer brand
    reputation is one of the top factors a candidate uses to
    assess if an organization will be the right fit for them.
    As an employer, you should also assess your candidate's
    online reputation in order to judge whether they are
    the candidate they claim to be on their resume. If the
    candidate is as trustworthy and reliable as they claim to
    be, their online presence should reflect that and there
    should not be anything countering what they have
    been sharing with you about their work experience.
    According to a 2018 CareerBuilder survey, 70% of
    employers use social media to screen candidates during
    the hiring process, and about 43% of employers use
    social media to check on current employees.[11] And
    according to the statistics, researching a prospective
    candidate online can literally change your opinion of
    the candidate: 54% of employers surveyed said they
    chose *not* to hire a candidate based on content found
    on their social media profile(s).[12] Some of the top
    reasons given for not hiring a candidate based on their
    online reputation include posting inappropriate
    photos or videos; posting information about drinking
    or using drugs; making discriminatory comments
    related to race, gender, or religion; bad-mouthing a

previous company or fellow employee; lying about qualifications; having poor communication skills; being linked to criminal behaviour; sharing confidential information from previous employers; and lying about an absence. Don't skip on researching your prospective employees online because this will help establish how transparent and trustworthy they really are.

- **Pay attention to candidates' body language and tone of voice**

  Candidates' body language and tone of voice can reveal a lot more about them than the words they use during the interview process. In the 1970s, Professor Albert Mehrabian of the University of California in Los Angeles found that words, tone of voice, and body language respectively account for 7%, 38%, and 55% of personal communication. Mehrabian added, 'The non-verbal elements are particularly important for communicating feelings and attitude, especially when they are incongruent: if words and body language disagree, one tends to believe the body language.'[13] What this study tells us is that non-verbal communication including body language and tone of voice are extremely valuable cues about the person communicating. When looking to hire a transparent employee, employers should pay close attention to the non-verbal communication of the candidate during the interview process. One key element to look for is incongruence, which is the lack of consistency between what the candidate says with their words and what their body language and tone of voice are communicating. For example, if the candidate says that they have consistently achieved their goals with their previous employer but they are not making eye contact with you, their tone of voice lacks confidence, and they are nervously tapping with their fingers on their desk, you might notice that what they say doesn't seem to match with how they say it. If that is the case, you should probably ask some follow-up questions to dig deeper. Some non-verbal communication red flags you should pay particular attention to include covering their mouth with their hand, repeatedly touching their nose, repeatedly scratching their neck or eyes, maintaining an unusually strong eye contact, or looking away repeatedly. Of course, non-verbal communication is not an exact science and you should use your intuition as well as the context when reading a candidate's body language and tone of voice during an interview. However, paying close attention to a prospective candidate's non-verbal cues during an interview can help you assess their transparency and trustworthiness.

The good news is that even in a hybrid work setting, where it is not always possible to interview candidates in person, you can still assess a candidate's transparency remotely. Checking candidates' references, giving them a pre-employment assessment, researching them online and paying attention to their body language and tone of voice can be done effectively remotely. Attracting transparent candidates is even more important in a hybrid work environment because employees need to know they can trust their colleagues regardless of whether they work in the same office or not.

While assessing your candidate's transparency during the hiring process, if you truly want to attract and retain transparent employees, you should also work to build a transparent employer brand. Intentionally developing a transparent employer brand will also help you attract and retain transparent employees. Your reputation as an employer and what your previous, current, and future employees think of you is what constitutes your employer brand. The more transparent and trustworthy you appear as an employer, the more you will attract and retain transparent and trustworthy employees.

A poor employer brand with a secretive reputation will prevent you from attracting and retaining transparent employees. One way to build an attractive and transparent employer brand is to leverage company review platforms such as Glassdoor. Glassdoor is a website where current and previous employees can anonymously review employers. Other websites, such as Comparably or Indeed, also offer employees the opportunity to rate their employers. By actively using these platforms and updating your company information, you will increase the chances of building an authentic employer brand that will attract and retain trustworthy employees that can relate to your company values. Leveraging social media platforms is another powerful way to create a transparent and attractive employer brand. Ensure that you regularly share stories on your social media channels about the day-to-day life at your

> A clear and authentic employer brand that is built on the value of transparency will not only attract but also retain transparent candidates.

company. Share pictures and videos of your team celebrating company milestones or celebrating someone's birthday. Use social media to make announcements about your organization. Engage with your company followers on social media as they interact with your posts. Participate in online conversations about your products and services so that you build trust online. Emphasize stories and announcements that showcase your company culture and core values to share an authentic look at what it's like to work for your organization. Communicate clearly about your core company values and your company culture with your existing employees as well through internal company emails and Slack messages. Discuss the importance of transparency with your existing employees, as they become your company's brand ambassadors and will also refer to their friends as potential candidates if they feel connected to your company's values.

The more unique and authentic your communication is with members of the public, the more your employer brand will stand out as unique and authentic and attract and retain transparent people who value your company's transparency. There is no one-size-fits-all way to communicate transparently about your employer brand, and there are many different ways to do so; the most important element to remember is to proactively think about your employer brand's transparency and to act on it as often as possible. The more time and effort you spend communicating externally and internally about your company's transparency, the more you will create transparency and the more you will attract and retain transparent people. Creating transparency and trust in your organization with prospective candidates is a two-way street. Just like in a relationship, you must be intentional about building trust with your brand ambassadors and with prospective employees. By nurturing a transparent image internally and externally, you are attracting the type of employees who deeply value transparency, and this will be a key factor of your success as an organization. As a hybrid organization with some employees working in the office, some employees working from home, some employees working both from the office and from home ,and some employees spread around the world, attracting and retaining transparent employees is becoming more essential than ever before because without transparency and trust, you will struggle with communication, collaboration, engagement, and productivity. Remember to prioritize communicating about transparency to attract and retain transparent people.

Encourage Leaders to Embrace Social Media

When Richard Branson published his autobiography *Finding My Virginity* in 2017, he talked openly about the huge role social media played in the success of his company. Branson recalls starting his Twitter account and his blog to connect with people and to highlight causes he cares passionately about, including boardroom diversity and ocean conservation. Branson recalls 'We've basically started our own in-house, online publishing operation, and thanks to social media I'm back in the editor's chair.' The business magnate recognized early on how important social media was for customer service, which is something that was always a key differentiator at Virgin. Branson recalls that in 2008, he received a letter from an unhappy customer that is now referred to as the 'funniest complaint letter of all time'. The customer didn't enjoy his meal on a Virgin flight and famously wrote to Richard, 'Well, answer me this, Richard, what sort of animal would serve a dessert with peas in? How can you live like this? I can't imagine what dinner round your house is like; it must be like something out of a nature documentary.' When Branson read the letter, he immediately called the team in charge of menus to ask they be changed back to top standard. He then called the unhappy customer to apologize and shared that his funny letter made him laugh. This story spread like wildfire on social media. Today, this story can still be found online as reported in many different online media outlets including Metro.co.uk under the title 'The five best customer complaint letters of all time'. When business leaders embrace social media in an authentic way to connect with their customers, beautiful things happen. Not only do customers and members of the public appreciate the brand more but business leaders connect with their customers in more meaningful ways. This strategy seems to be working well for Virgin, as Virgin Media's employee engagement score was 79% in 2019.[14]

Richard Branson and Virgin are not an exception, as there are many other business leaders who have fully embraced social media. Sara Blakely, founder and CEO of Spanx, is arguably one of the most influential business leaders and someone who has fully embraced social media as a platform of choice to connect with members of the public. Named in *Time* magazine's 'Time 100' annual list of the 100 most influential people in the world, Sara Blakely founded the now internationally recognized shapewear company Spanx in 2000. In 2012, Blakely was named the youngest self-made billionaire by *Forbes*. Sara Blakely admitted herself that she is 'the DNA' of her company. Her personality is a big part of Spanx's marketing. Sara has mastered the art of social media by sharing honest behind-the-scenes moments of both her personal life and her company Spanx. Sara comes across as approachable and relatable, whilst giving prospective employees a sneak peek at what it's like to work at Spanx. Sara also shares important life lessons on social media that inspire both her customers and her employees. She often talks openly about letting go of fear, loosening up, and using humour. Sara Blakely's Instagram account is full of engaging insights and tips for business owners and entrepreneurs. Her stories are very relatable, honest, and helpful. Sara uses a lot of funny stories and humour to match her personal style. Clearly, embracing social media has been working well for Sara because she gained 1.5 million followers on LinkedIn, and was named among the 100 most powerful women in the world by *Forbes* in 2015.

If you are more of an introvert and usually keep your personal life separate from your work life, you can still use social media in a way that is both authentic and meaningful. You don't need to share family holiday pictures or videos of your morning run if this doesn't feel natural to you. However, as a business leader, you should definitely use social media platforms regularly to connect with your customers, employees, and members of the public, and to build extreme transparency. There are many benefits to the organization when business leaders embrace social media platforms:

- **It creates a transparent environment**
  When CEOs post LinkedIn updates, employees at all levels in the organization feel that their CEO is accessible and also more relatable. Everyone values

open communication because it creates trust, transparency, and rapport. Customers also prefer a CEO who often shares updates on social media rather than a secretive CEO who never shares anything, because they are more likely to trust a CEO who is fully present and who often shares information. Overtime, CEOs who share updates often on social media gain a better brand reputation, which benefits the organization.

- **It sets the tone**
  Business leaders' attitudes online and offline influence employees' attitudes, as well as customers' attitudes and most people around them. This is because business leaders hold a position of authority, and what they say, do, and how they act is often regarded as the standard by the people around them. So when CEOs, managing directors, or vice presidents share an update on social media, what they say and how they say it often becomes what their employees will say and how their employees behave. The most influential leaders such as Richard Branson, Sara Blakely, and Arianna Huffington all share a positive attitude on social media. Richard brings his fun and upbeat attitude, Sara shares her inspiring energy and humorous tone, and Arianna brings her wisdom and shares her positive habits on social media. As a result, they all run successful organizations that have often been voted the best places to work, best customer service, or both!

- **It provides direct and honest feedback**
  When business leaders embrace social media, one of the benefits is that they will automatically receive feedback. Customers, prospects, and other members of

the public usually comment on CEOs' social media posts. From customer complaints to customer praises, from prospective customers' questions about a product or service, to prospective employees' comments, many people will engage with the conversion online. This is a good thing because it keeps the conversation going and it provides a unique opportunity to act on customer and prospective customer's feedback on areas for improvement. Much more cost effective and direct than a formal customer poll, social media feedback can help your organization improve your products and services, sell more, and improve customer satisfaction.

- **It boosts employee engagement**

    When Richard Branson successfully completed Virgin Galactic's first space flight, one of the first things he did when coming back was to share an online praise about his team:

'Life is all about people, and so are businesses – even the world's first commercial spaceline. From the astonishingly calm and skilful pilots Mark "Forger" Stucky and CJ Sturckow – now astronauts – to the talented and diligent ground crews and support teams. From the people who have worked behind the scenes over the 14 years of Virgin Galactic and The Spaceship Company's journey so far, to the people supporting us from the flightline and all around the globe.'[15]

Branson also famously shared on Twitter: 'Be kind, praise more than criticise and you might change somebody's life and make a huge positive difference to your business too.' Praising employees on social media

boosts employee morale, encourages peer-to-peer
support and fosters a culture of praise.

- **It helps connect with employees and customers**
Most people use social media as a way to connect
with others. When you are the leader of a team or an
organization, you also get an opportunity to connect
with people through social media. Leaders who engage
with other people's comments, questions, and feedback
develop a rapport with these people and with their
community. Social media is a two-way street and
requires listening and responding to what others are
saying online. When business leaders invest their time
and energy into engaging on social media, they develop
rapport and connect with employees and customers in
a more meaningful way, which creates more
transparency and trust.

If your leadership team is not sure where to start with
social media, here is a guide that can help them:

- **Share valuable information for your customers**
Start by sharing content that actually adds value
for your customers. Focus on helping your prospects
and customers improve their work or life by giving
them tips and tools that will actually help them. This
can be done with any format of your choice, whether
you share video content, a blog post, a news article, a
research paper, a survey, a white paper, or any other
form of content, as long as you provide value to your
audience. Many business leaders who have no
experience with social media tend to focus on the
benefits of their products and services, or why their
brand is superior to others. That strategy is very
self-driven and doesn't add any value to their audience.

Instead, focus on helping your community in any way, shape, or form. This will organically build trust with your customer base because they will respond to the value you bring to their life, and you will also build credibility and thought leadership within your community.

- **Read and respond to people's reactions**

  Social media is a two-way communication; it is not just a platform to speak publicly. Social media users want meaningful connection online, so you should focus on building engagement. Connecting with customers online also builds brand loyalty. Read users' comments and respond to some of these. Take the time to follow some of your customers on social media, read their posts, and react to their posts. This also demonstrates that you actually care about your customers and prospects because you read their posts and respond to them. Ed Bastian, CEO of Delta Airlines, often comments on other people's posts on LinkedIn. This strategy is clearly working for him, as he has accumulated more than 210,667 followers on LinkedIn, and even his employees respond well, as 90% of his employees approve of him, according to Glassdoor.

- **Focus on company culture**

  As one of the most influential CEOs on social media demonstrates, talking about company culture can significantly boost transparency and build trust in the brand. Jeff Weiner, LinkedIn's long-term CEO who recently became LinkedIn executive chairman, often shares insights about his company culture on social media. In one recent LinkedIn post, Weiner shared a

view from the LinkedIn office in San Francisco and
accumulated thousands of likes and many comments.
Weiner also understands the importance of engaging
with his employees' posts on social media, because it
demonstrates his enthusiasm for the company culture
and its people. Remember that your leader's use of
social media is like a window to your company
culture so your leaders should spend a lot of time
sharing what your company culture is like. This
improves your employer branding and builds trust for
your brand for prospective employees and customers.

- **Be authentic**
  Another key aspect of leveraging social media to
  build transparency is to be authentic, according to Jeff
  Weiner: 'It comes down to authenticity; authentically
  communicate what you are most passionate about,
  what inspires you, and what you've learned or
  experienced that others can benefit from.' He
  continued, 'The more authentic you can be, the more
  effective you will be.' As the leader of one of the most
  successful social media companies, Weiner understands
  what it takes to create a strong social media presence
  that has a big impact. The more you share on social
  media, the more the public will recognize your
  authentic voice and the more you will be able to
  connect with them. The more you practise sharing on
  social media, the more you will find your authentic
  voice, so you need to dedicate a set amount of time
  each day to social media. Start with what you are
  comfortable sharing and build on it; the more you
  share, the more natural it will become for you to share

and be authentic and this will resonate with your community.

Encouraging your leaders to embrace social media can feel like a daunting task and can seem disconnected from achieving success. Many business leaders are not very active on social media and simply share content from their company's official social media pages. Some business leaders perceive social media as not business critical, and the majority of CEOs and C-suite executives have never been taught how to leverage social media platforms anyway. However, the world we live in has changed dramatically since the days many CEOs started their career, and in a hybrid work environment where online presence is more scrutinized than ever before, modern CEOs and business leaders can no longer afford to be invisible on social media. Customers, prospective customers, employees, prospective employees, and members of the public are looking for business leaders who share openly about their company culture, their vision, and who actively engage with their community online.

> Having company leaders actively sharing and engaging online with their community is no longer a 'nice-to-have'. It is becoming a business priority in a hybrid work environment because attracting and retaining top talent and customers starts online by building a transparent employer brand that is authentic and inspires trust. Trust is the foundation to any business relationship.

As Jeff Weiner famously said: 'I've come to learn there is a virtuous cycle to transparency and a very vicious cycle of obfuscation.' This could not be more true in a hybrid world where employees and customers spend more time on social media than ever before. Businesses whose leaders are embracing social media in an authentic way are winning trust and building extreme transparency faster and better than those whose leaders are invisible on social media.

Promote Open Communication

When Ray Dalio, chairman of the world's largest hedge fund Bridgewater Associates, whose net worth is about $20 billion, is asked about the reason for his success, his answer is: 'radical transparency'. Dalio explains:

> 'I want independent thinkers who are going to disagree. The most important things I want are meaningful work and meaningful relationships. And I believe that the way to get those is through radical truth and radical transparency. In order to be successful, we have to have independent thinkers – so independent that they'll bet against the consensus. You have to put your honest thoughts on the table. Then, the best ideas rise to the top.'

Ray Dalio's open communication philosophy has always been a key factor to his success and what led his company to become the largest hedge fund firm in the world. Dalio's open communication approach is highlighted on his company's website: 'Bridgewater's competitive edge is our pioneering workplace culture that relies on truthful and transparent communication to ensure the best ideas win out.' Dalio further explains his 'principled approach' on his company website: 'With the goal of creating an idea meritocracy, Ray wrote a set of principles that became the framework for the firm's management philosophy. Chief among them is employing radical truth and radical transparency – encouraging open and honest dialogue and allowing the best thinking to prevail.' Building radical transparency and open communication allows for honest discussions and a free flow of ideas which leads to the best outcome. Promoting open communication creates psychological safety where everyone feels safe to share their ideas without fear of being ridiculed. This allows for more creative thinking and innovation, which gives the organization a competitive advantage.

Open communication at work happens when every employee in an organization is empowered to share their ideas in a safe environment. Each employee is able to express their ideas to each other and to debate freely on any topic. It happens when information is shared between all employees in a transparent and consistent way. Team members are assertive and are encouraged to express their thoughts and feelings clearly in an open-minded environment.

Creating a culture of openness at work promotes clarity. Employees are clear on what the goals are and what the business is working on. Teams understand what the overall mission is and how to work better with each other.

Promoting an open communication approach has many benefits to the business and is an essential part of building extreme transparency at work.

Each employee is more connected to the company's values and vision. Promoting open communication at work also fosters employee engagement. When the CEO and business leaders ask for the opinion of different people, they send the message that they care about what their employees think. No opinion is more important than another, and no role should weigh more than another. This makes employees feel valued, heard and respected, and it creates a stronger sense of belonging. Fostering open communication at work also boosts company performance because the goal is no longer to be right but to find the best decision for the business. It removes any politics or confidential projects and creates a culture of winning together as one team. Open communication also fosters innovation because everyone shares their ideas and creative thinking, instead of just a few employees. Every employee, every team, and every department is more likely to innovate often because all ideas are equally weighed, and the best ideas win instead of just the ideas of the most senior employees. An open communication approach also improves employee retention because employees feel respected and heard when they are asked to share their ideas often.

Culture Amp analysed data from over 150 companies and over 60 000 employees to study what drives employee engagement in their New Tech Benchmark survey.[16] The survey revealed that out of the top ten factors driving employee engagement, three are related to good communication:

- Employees feel happy with their current role relative to what was described to them.
- Leaders have communicated a vision that motivates employees.

- Employees experience open and honest two-way communication.

Likewise, the factors that dictate whether employees are disengaged at work all relate to communication, according to the same Culture Amp survey. The following factors are the ones driving the most employee engagement or disengagement:

- Effectively directing resources towards company goals.
- Leaders who inspire confidence.
- Leaders that demonstrate people are important to the company's success.
- Leaders that communicate a motivating vision.

In her book *Radical Candor: How to Get What You Want by Saying What You Mean*, Kim Scott introduced the idea of being radically candid or transparent in our communication at work in order to be successful. She writes: 'When bosses are too invested in everyone getting along, they also fail to encourage the people on their team to criticize one another for fear of sowing discord. They create the kind of work environment where being "nice" is prioritized at the expense of critiquing and therefore improving actual performance.' Scott also said, 'Jobs articulated this approach more gently in an interview with Terry Gross: "At Apple we hire people to tell us what to do, not the other way around."'

Although the concept of being open and transparent and communicating freely might seem scary for some leaders, the benefits truly outweigh the risks. Communicating freely without fear of criticism builds a positive work environment where people feel safe and valued; in contrast, restricting communication to a few people in the organization and only sharing limited information creates an environment with no trust and a lack of motivation for employees who want to share their ideas and feel valued.

As Ray Dalio recalls, his radical transparency approach to communication was not always well understood by his early team members. Dalio recalls that in 1993, three of his closest collaborators told him that he was being 'too honest'. They sent him a note reading: 'Ray sometimes says or does things to employees which makes them feel incompetent, unnecessary, humiliated, overwhelmed, belittled, pressed, or otherwise bad. If he doesn't manage people well, growth will be stunted and we will all be affected.' Dalio recalls that the feedback stayed with him ever since. So he decided to meet individually with his team to come to a mutual agreement about how they should communicate. He wanted to create a culture where everyone could have 'thoughtful disagreements' and discuss their ideas without creating problems. That event led him to create his now well-known 'principles' to create a radical transparent culture. Ray Dalio himself is an example of transparency, especially when he publicly shared an email that one of his employees sent him, which read as follows:

'Ray – you deserve a "D–" for your performance today in the meeting. . . you did not prepare at all because there is no way you could have and been that disorganized. In the future, I/we would ask you to take some time and prepare and maybe even I should come up and start talking to you to get you warmed up or something, but we can't let this happen again. If you in any way think my view is wrong, please ask the others or we can talk about it.' Instead of being offended, Dalio took that email as an example of how employees should speak to each other. As Dalio himself said, 'In order to be successful, we have to have independent thinkers – so independent that they'll bet against the consensus. And to do that, you have to put your honest thoughts on the table.' Then, the best ideas rise to the top.

Promoting a culture of open communication takes time, effort, and a strategy. In a hybrid work environment, where most employees are never in the same location as their co-workers, building an open communication culture becomes more important than ever before to ensure that everyone is working collaboratively. Remote workers in particular need to be in the know and also to be able to voice their opinions just as much, if not more than, in-office workers. Here is how to promote an open communication culture in hybrid work:

- **Host open meetings**
  Hosting meetings where some participants are in the office and some are joining remotely can present some challenges when it comes to open communication. Remote participants may struggle to join in the conversation and to get in the debate. Office participants may forget about remote participants and get carried away without offering remote participants a chance to join in the discussion. To avoid leaving any participant out when hosting hybrid meetings, you might implement a few simple rules and reinforce the rules during all your meetings. Implement a round-robin rule where each participant takes turns to speak. One of the most efficient ways to ensure this happens is to appoint a dedicated meeting host. Your meeting host is responsible for ensuring that each participant

gets equal speaking time. Your meeting host should also be on the lookout for group dynamics such as any off-topic question asked only to test the presenter, or any passive-aggressive comment. They should set the tone for your meetings and redirect discussions to the main topics and ensure everyone gets a chance to contribute equally to the discussion. Another powerful way to host open meetings that foster open communication in hybrid work is to avoid the use of chats during meetings. Chats during meetings can be very distracting and take the attention away from the presenter. Meeting participants should be encouraged to speak up if they have any question or feedback during the meeting, so that everyone can hear them and focus on what is being said rather than being distracted by the chat conversation.

- **Prioritize networking**
  The number of employees who have never met their colleagues face-to-face has drastically increased since Covid. A large number of employees who started a new job since the start of the Covid pandemic have never met their co-workers in person. Remote work and hybrid work make it harder for employees to get to know each other, to build rapport and trust and to create an environment where open communication is the norm. This is why it is so important to focus on networking and team building as often as possible. Networking can be as simple as starting any meeting with some icebreaker questions for the participants. Icebreaker questions in meetings can range from an update on the weekend, to hobbies, to holiday plans, etc.

Talking about people's interests outside of work will open up interesting conversations and literally break the ice in your teams.

Wherever possible, try to schedule some networking and team-building time face-to-face, as this is the most powerful way to build rapport. If face-to-face team building is not possible, hosting virtual networking meetings are a fun way to build rapport, trust, and an open communication culture in your team.

- **Frequent check-ins and open-door policy**

  Managers who frequently check in with their people are the ones who really set the tone for an open communication culture. Ensure that you regularly check in with as many co-workers as possible by setting up regular cadence meetings with them. Managers who prioritize contacting the people in their teams and departments often are the ones who truly build an open communication culture. Team leaders who create an open-door policy build an open communication culture as well as transparency in their teams, and they encourage free-flowing communication. Sending a simple email to your team to say that you are available between 9 a.m. and 12 p.m. for catch-ups will encourage people to call you and discuss any topic they want to. Another way to encourage an open-door culture is to invite people to add colleagues during meetings when needed. You can send an email to say that if your colleagues are having a meeting and they realize they need another colleague's input, they should get into the habit of calling that colleague in the moment.

This is what an open-door policy looks like in a virtual world: simply getting into the habit of dialling in a colleague when in the middle of a meeting. These simple actions send the message that your team is always open to discussion, no matter where the people are based or what people's job titles are. And if the managers themselves adopt these habits, usually the team embraces the culture even faster.

Promoting open communication in your organization might seem uncomfortable at first, especially if you have never operated this way before. You might feel outside of your comfort zone initially and wonder if you might run into any challenges related to sharing confidential information, trust issues, or creating unwanted conflict. However, this fear of running into challenges is really an illusion because withdrawing information is exactly what creates trust issues and unresolved conflicts, especially when people feel left out and excluded from conversations, which is what leads to resentment and bad feelings.

> Embrace open communication by hosting open meetings where everyone has an equal opportunity to contribute. By prioritizing networking, checking in frequently, and encouraging an open-door policy, and you will build extreme transparency in your team and organization.

If you operate in a virtual or hybrid work environment, your team will become more confident and collaborative when they feel like the culture is focused on open communication. As Ray

Dalio wrote in his best-selling book *Principles: Life and Work*, 'The most meaningful relationships are achieved when you and others can speak openly to each other about everything that's important, learn together, and understand the need to hold each other accountable to be as excellent as you can be.'

Create a Flatter Organization

When Billy Seeney, design lead at Squarespace, was asked what makes his team structure effective, his answer was the flat structure:

> 'We've changed our structure a fair amount over the years as we've grown – we're always looking for the most effective organization. Our mostly flat structure allows each of us to work on the things we're passionate about, which gives the team room to shift around as different needs surface. We recently evened out the number of direct reports that each manager has, which helped a lot in putting together an efficient team. In a great creative culture, people feel free to share ideas, opinions, and criticisms.'

His colleague Danni Fisher, product designer at Squarespace, added,

> 'This year, we introduced a product design weekly sync led by our Director of Product Design. The meeting is loosely formatted and gives an opportunity for each designer to share his or her work and thoughts on the creative process. We

aren't timeboxed and it doesn't matter what work is presented – the most important aspect is that each team member has the opportunity to share something. Collectively, we offer critiques and ideas to help teammates think through a particular problem they may be stuck on. The transparency that comes with sharing our work and thought process is key.'

When asked about the culture at Squarespace, Billy adds:

'Our leadership team plays a major role in establishing the company culture by way of hiring decisions, communication styles, and opportunities given to employees. Our CEO sits right next to us, in the same kind of chair, at the same custom concrete desk, with the same computer equipment everyone else has. This sends a profound message to the company about equality of ideas, and the fact that he's not tucked away in a glass office somewhere in a suit speaks volumes to the entire organization.'

A flat organizational structure like the Squarespace culture is increasingly becoming relevant in a hybrid work environment. This is because flat structures promote a degree of trust and openness that are especially important in a remote work or hybrid work environment. Trust has never been more important to the success of teams in a virtual work environment and having a flat structure promotes trust. The structure of an organization helps employees understand how they are connected to one another, so having a flat structure sends the message that every employee is as important as anyone else and is as connected to the CEO as any other employee, promoting openness, trust, and collaboration. Virtual and hybrid teams are more successful in a flatter organization for many reasons. When teams are decentralized and physically separated, work is better done in a decentralized structure. As McKinsey explains, 'When the workforce is hybrid virtual, leaders need to rely less on hierarchical and more on inspirational forms of leadership. The dispersed employees working remotely require new leadership behaviors to compensate for the reduced socioemotional cues characteristic of digital channels.'[17]

So what exactly is a flat organizational structure? A flat structure refers to an organization with very few levels of management between leadership and employees. The flat organization emphasizes each employee's accountability and their involvement in decision-making. Some flat organizations have no middle managers, and decisions can be made by self-organizing teams or by rotating managers. Some flat organizations have only a few managers who are responsible for larger teams. All flat organizations have significantly less management layers than traditional hierarchical structures. Flat organizations present many benefits to teams, especially in a hybrid work environment where every employee is more isolated and needs to be able to make their own decisions quickly.

First and foremost, communication improves significantly in a flatter organization. Information can flow freely between all the different employees and departments, silos are removed. Employees are empowered to go and look for the information they need directly from the source without having to wait for authorization or fear of bypassing a manager. There is less room for miscommunication, as everyone gets access to the information they need directly from the sources. Information is also much more immediate and there is less delay caused by unnecessary waiting times.

Second, employees feel more empowered and engaged through the increased autonomy and trust they gain from a flatter structure. Employees no longer feel that they are being micromanaged and told what to do and how to do their job. Employees feel they are being treated as adults and empowered to do their work to the best of their ability. The entire energy of the organization is more positive and creative, as employees no longer feel stopped in their tracks by unnecessary processes. Employee engagement and motivation rises with a flatter structure.

Third, innovation happens faster and more often in a flatter organization. Innovation comes from experimentation and when every employee is free to do what they think is right, more employees experiment with new ways of working, which in turn, leads to more innovation at every level of the organization. Innovation is no longer the remit of the Research and Development department or the Engineering team but becomes everyone's remit.

Finally, flatter structures are much more cost-effective than traditional hierarchical structures. Middle managers are usually expensive, and when they are no longer needed, the organization can enjoy significant cost savings that they would otherwise not be able to enjoy.

So what steps can you take to revisit your company structure and create a flatter organization?

- **Remove unnecessary middle management layers**

    Make an audit of your middle management layer and remove as many middle managers as possible from your organization chart. You might repurpose their role to individual contributor roles whenever relevant. These intermediate managers and team leaders effectively remove initiative, empowerment, and autonomy from the individual contributors they manage, whether this is intentional or not. The simple fact of having many layers of middle managers sends the message that individual contributors are not fully empowered to make decisions. This also means that the flow of information between individual contributors and the leadership team is not free, and it blocks the communication internally. McKinsey pointed out that in truly agile organizations, we often see only three layers of management.[18] The more direct communication is, the more transparency exists.

    > Allowing more direct communication between all individual contributors and the leadership team fosters transparency.

    In a hybrid work environment, where most communication takes place online, employees who feel empowered to make their own decisions and to speak directly with the leadership team are more likely to feel trusted than if they have to constantly go through their direct managers to get approvals.

- **Empower front-line employees to get involved with the leadership team**

    Employees who are individual contributors a often are those who actually deal with the customers, prospects, vendors, and members of the public on a daily basis. These front-line workers often have much more qualitative information, knowledge, and understanding about the customers and the ecosystem than executive teams. In any case, these employees who are on the ground hold a lot of extremely valuable information. Creating opportunities for front-line employees to speak directly with the leadership team is a key factor to creating a flatter organization that fosters extreme transparency. In a hybrid work environment, hosting regular all-hands meetings that are hosted by individual contributors can be a powerful way to achieve extreme transparency and to let information flow from employees who are 'on the ground'. Creating communication channels where every individual contributor is encouraged to participate is another powerful way to create that direct line of communication between individual contributors and leadership teams.

- **Delegate decision-making to everyone**
  One of the key elements of a successful flat organization is delegating decision-making to every individual contributor. A successful flat organization has clearly defined roles and responsibilities, a mission, a vision, clear values, and has delegated responsibility to every employee. Each employee feels trusted to make the best decision for the organization, without any need to request approvals. When decision-making is delegated, the entire organization becomes more agile, and the team becomes more motivated because everyone knows they are trusted to make the right decisions. There is no more micromanagement, and

everyone trusts their co-workers to make the right decisions for the organization.

In 2019, the CEO of digital marketing agency Jellyfish took a big step when he decided to remove senior managers and heads of departments from his organization structure. Rob Pierre, who had been the co-founder and CEO of Jellyfish since 2005, came to the realization that the traditional hierarchical organization chart encouraged the wrong type of behaviour. Pierre admits that the heavy management layers were blocking productivity, so he replaced senior managers and heads of departments with steering groups of employees where responsibilities were shared. One of the many interesting changes that happened when Jellyfish became a flatter organization is that the promotions were handled differently. Every employee had a chance to present a business case for their promotion, which were anonymized and judged by a panel of employees. Since that system was implemented, more than 800 employees have been promoted and 57% of these are women. Pierre believes that this anonymization of the promotion process helped reduce unconscious bias and promote more gender equality. Pierre also believes that his company's flat organization model can be used successfully by any organization and his advice is to 'focus on your desired outcomes, get everyone in leadership to become an advocate – and address any reservations immediately'.

In order to make a flatter organization work in a remote work model or hybrid work environment, leaders will need to shift their approach to leadership. Leaders who might have been outstanding leaders in a face-to-face office environment may have to adapt and evolve to a remote-first environment in order to be successful. Here are a few leadership skills that should be embraced in order to build a successful flat organization in a hybrid work environment:

- **Role modelling more than before**

  Now that you operate in a hybrid work environment as a leader, your interactions with your co-workers, which are rarer than before, become scrutinized even more than they were previously in an office environment. This is because your people have fewer opportunities to see you and interact with you, and when they do, they will pay even more attention to how you show up. In a flatter organization, leaders continue to be in a position of authority and influence; therefore, their approach will be mirrored by their people. For example, if you work in a hybrid work environment but you are in the office five days a week, you are sending the message that people should be in the office. Instead, you should work as many days remotely as you do in the office, sending the message that you support a hybrid work environment.

- **Become an inspirational leader**

  In a flat organization, there are fewer middle managers and heads of departments, but the leadership team remains present as the guide on how to operate. So in order to build a flat organization that will succeed, the senior leadership team should work on becoming an inspiring leadership team that lifts people up and celebrates employee empowerment. For example, leaders should embrace opportunities to mentor some employees to show their support and availability. Leaders might also consider embracing their authentic voice to show that the company celebrates every employee's individuality.

- **Leading through consensus**

As the organization becomes flatter and the team continues to be geographically distributed, it is important that leaders transition from a traditional 'command and control' leadership approach to a 'consensus-led' approach.

Many senior leaders have worked for decades using the traditional command and control method, where they make the decisions and expect the team to follow blindly. However, this approach will no longer work in a flatter organization, and everyone needs to make the mental shift from a traditional top-down leadership approach to a modern bottom-up and consensus-led approach. For instance, leaders should often ask open questions in team meetings and listen and take notes. They might start using surveys more often to get more quantitative feedback from their people. The key is to invite everyone's voices in a flatter organization and to make group decisions.

Creating a flatter organization in a hybrid work environment will truly build an additional layer of transparency and trust that will lead to better performance. When middle management layers are removed and replaced by steering groups, everyone feels more heard and valued, especially in a distributed team where many people work remotely. This approach to work fosters more collaboration, more trust, and ultimately more transparency. Empowering front-line employees to get involved with the leadership team, including remote workers, and delegating decision-making to everyone truly builds more trust and transparency in the organization, which leads to better collaboration and performance. As Bill Gates himself said, 'The flatter the corporate hierarchy, the more likely it is that employees will communicate bad news and act upon it.'[19]

Create Employee–to–Leadership Communication Channels

In 2020, leading British multinational retailer Marks & Spencer (M&S) had recently launched a programme to get employees to share their ideas via email with their CEO Steve Rowe. However, some M&S employees were not using emails regularly, and using emails to manage ideas was proving very challenging and tedious. The company needed a way to better engage more employees in the conversation with their CEO. This is when the company adopted a new way to create a communication channel between all employees and the CEO: in 2021, M&S launched an app called 'Suggest to Steve' that allowed employees to share their ideas directly with their CEO, from their mobile phone or from their desktops. Employees could also like and comment on other employees' ideas, which increased communication and transparency. Moving from traditional emails to an app increased the volume of ideas by 70% year-on-year, and employee engagement is reported to be higher than ever with over 3000 ideas, likes, and comments being shared every single month.[20] When Covid-19 hit, Michaela, an M&S employee, used the app to share her idea with her CEO: she suggested that the company raise money to support the National Health Service (NHS). Michaela's idea was heard by her CEO Steve, who decided to embrace it. They raised over £150 000! Opening a dedicated communication channel for employees to speak directly with their CEO built a more transparent environment and gave employees a voice that they previously didn't have.

M&S is not the only company who has mastered exceptional employee-to-leadership communication. Google is well known for its transparency when it comes to sharing information internally with all employees. In contrast to M&S, Google doesn't use an app; they use a weekly all-hands meeting to allow any employee to speak directly with the co-founders Larry Page and Sergey Brin. Every employee at Google is invited to join that meeting, which can happen either in person or in a video format, and anyone can ask a question during the dedicated Q&A session, which is by far the most important part of that meeting. Another way that Google fosters full transparency is by giving newly hired software engineers access to almost all of their code on their first day.[21]

Leadership communication refers to the messages that are shared internally by the leadership team of an organization. These messages have a significant impact for the employees because they set the tone for the company culture and values of the organization. Good leadership communication with employees directly impacts the success of the organization. Creating direct employee-to-leadership communication channels is critical to building extreme transparency in the organization. Employee-to-leadership communication channels are the means by which workers can directly communicate with their leader, in a two-way communication approach. The communication channels used have a direct impact on employees' feelings of belonging and inclusion in the organization. Effective employee-to-leadership communication channels should be more informal to encourage everyone to participate. They should allow employees to participate in a relaxed environment without fear of being judged or criticized. Ideally, these channels should enable conversations in a friendly environment.

In a hybrid work environment, these communication channels can take different forms. Face-to-face communication is still important to bring the human element to it and is also great for team building. However, this is not always possible in a hybrid work environment; instead, organizations can host hybrid communication channels where the CEO can be in the office with some office workers in a conference room and some employees can join remotely. In that scenario, it is important to pay extra attention to remote workers and make sure they are actively being invited and included in the conversation; this can be done in different ways including using a very large screen showing their faces to in-office attendees, having a meeting moderator who invites remote workers to ask questions, using a group chat before and during the meeting to allow remote workers to ask questions there, etc. In a hybrid work environment, employee-to-leadership communication channels can also take a digital form. Internal communication platforms such as Zoom meetings, or employee collaboration tools such as Slack channels, can also be used to facilitate conversations between the leadership team and employees. Some organizations might prefer to use fully digital communication channels instead of hybrid channels in order to make every employee feel equally heard and comfortable to participate in the discussion. The format of the employee-to-leadership communication channels might evolve over time as the organization evolves, and it is good practice to get feedback from employees about their preferred communication channel. There is a wide variety of communication channels that organizations can choose from, depending on the company culture and the employees' preferred choice of communication. These include the intranet, emails, project management tools, newsletters, messaging software, video conferencing software such as Zoom, internal podcasts, company blogs, employee feedback softwares, internal social media channels, and employee survey solutions. Regardless of which communication channel is used, it is important that it allows two-way communication between the leadership team and employees.

When authors Boris Groysberg and Michael Slind conducted research on effective leadership, they found that there are four main elements of effective leadership in an organization, in particular when it comes to leadership communication: intimacy, interactivity, inclusion, and intentionality. The authors found that intimacy helps move from a traditional top-down approach to a more engaging bottom-up exchange.[22] This can be achieved by using a less corporate and more casual tone. Interactivity is achieved through dialogue and giving way to a two-way exchange. Inclusion refers to empowering all employees to have a voice on company channels including on social media. Intentionality enables leaders to share key messages by explaining them rather than just enforcing them. By using these four key elements of leadership communication with employees, leaders can create a truly transparent work environment.

In a hybrid work environment, it can be particularly challenging to achieve effective employee-to-leadership communication because there are fewer opportunities to engage face-to-face with the CEO and the leadership team when not in the office. However, there are ways to achieve powerful employee-to-leadership communication even in a distributed work environment:

- **Supporting two-way communication**
  In a hybrid work environment, creating and sustaining two-way communication between the leadership team and employees is fundamental. The goal is to achieve an open dialogue between employees and the CEO. Listening is key, so make sure that you listen to your employees and act on the feedback you receive; this shows that you pay attention and that you truly care. This can be achieved by hosting a longer Q&A session in your weekly town hall meeting. This can also be achieved by hosting a special Q&A session based on the feedback you received in the previous town hall, as this shows that you listened and that you care, and you want to continue the discussion.

- **Asking for feedback and acting upon it**
  One powerful way to create extreme transparency in your organization through employee-to-leadership communication is getting leaders to proactively ask for feedback and act upon it. This can be achieved by creating a session in the weekly town hall meeting dedicated to 'giving CEO feedback'. The CEO could explain that they value employee feedback on the CEO's performance and invite employees to share such feedback. This is a great example of leadership communication focusing on employee feedback. If the setting is too intimidating and employees shy away

from sharing feedback in front of everyone, this can be done via a poll or survey, where employees answer a live poll online by using a tool such as Slido.com. Employees will still get a chance to share feedback about their CEO via the survey tool and they won't have to speak in front of everyone. The CEO could then discuss what they see from the survey; the point here is that the CEO is asking for employee feedback and is open to listening and discussing the feedback in front of everyone, demonstrating that they are open to a transparent dialogue.

- **Making information accessible**
  Even if your organization has an employee-to-leadership communication channel in place, it doesn't necessarily mean that the conversation will happen if important information is not shared with employees outside of the channel. If employees don't know where the organization is headed, what the latest decisions are, and when important events are happening, there won't be much discussion happening at all. It is important that the leadership team shares important company information often with all employees, in a way that makes it easy for employees to find where the information is. Ideally, the content should be shared in a single place for ease of use by all employees. This accessible information about the company will allow employees to feel involved and to prepare their questions for the leadership team ahead of time. This is particularly relevant in a hybrid work environment where employees are geographically dispersed and need easy access to important information about the company.

- **Be authentic**

    Leaders will have to embrace becoming even
more authentic in order to build that important layer
of trust in a hybrid work environment. Ever since the
Covid-19 pandemic, people have been craving
connection and rapport, including in the workplace.
Some leaders have successfully managed to be more
authentic and personal during this crisis, and they
have opened up doors to more meaningful discussions
and rapport in a remote or hybrid work environment.
Authentic leaders who communicate often to all
employees build more trust and transparency in the
organization and set the tone for what type of
relationships they want to see in their organizations.

- **Measure employee engagement**

    Whatever channel of communication you decide
to use for a direct employee-to-leadership discussion,
you should constantly measure employee engagement
in order to adjust your communication channel. For
instance, you might start with a weekly town hall
meeting with a 15-minute Q&A for all employees to
ask direct questions to the CEO, and you might notice
in your surveys that many employees feel intimidated
by the size of the group and therefore do not engage.
You might then offer a virtual chat to allow the more
introverted employees to ask questions online, and you
might see better engagement and involvement from
these employees. Or you might start by inviting
employees to share their suggestions with the CEO via
emails and through an employee survey. You might
notice that some employees do not participate because
the email might seem too complicated; you might then

decide to build an app for sharing ideas with the CEO, and you might see an increased participation rate from employees using this method. Remember to always measure employee engagement regarding your communication channel with leadership in order to constantly adjust and improve your communication channel accordingly.

When the Covid-19 pandemic forced companies to quickly change gear and adopt new ways of working, Deirdre Garvey, CEO of The Wheel, had to shift to remote working quickly, like many other organizations at the time. Garvey is now implementing a hybrid work model and shares that creating a 'single source of truth intranet' was one of the key initiatives they launched in order to build a successful hybrid team. Garvey explains, 'We now have a communication charter, a single source of truth intranet, we understand the importance of meta skills like empathy, creativity, self-awareness, flexibility, and cross skills.' Garvey also talks about the importance of communication between the leadership team and employees, as she says: 'Pay more attention to communication than you ever thought was reasonable', and 'Invest in training, treat your staff well, and listen'. She also adds: 'It will help you to be a better listener'.

> Creating great employee-to-leadership communication channels to build extreme transparency will help create the right conditions for teams to be successful in a distributed work environment.

Many organizations have not revisited their communication channels since the start of the

Covid-19 pandemic and are stuck in an old way of communicating, which is based on the 'command and control' approach. These companies are still operating using a top-down approach and are failing to adapt to the new way of working. Employees are hungrier than ever before for authentic communication and they want to have a voice in how the organization operates. Simply put, employees who feel connected to their co-workers and organizations report being more productive. Connection and a sense of belonging in hybrid work can only be achieved through good communication between employees and the leadership team. In order to build outstanding employee-to-leadership communication channels in hybrid work, organizations should support two-way communication where leaders listen as much as their employees; leaders should also ask for feedback and act upon it. Leaders should make important company information accessible, thrive to be authentic, and measure employee engagement. This can be achieved on social media channels as previously mentioned, but also in weekly company town hall meetings or through dedicated apps. Regardless of which communication channel is used, leaders should pay attention to what their employees are saying and should build dedicated communication channels that invite each and every employee to talk to them directly.

Conclusion

Distributed teams who spend less time face-to-face in an office tend to be less in the know of what is happening in the organization. This is because opportunities for spontaneous communication and information sharing are less frequent in a hybrid work environment. As a result, employees and teams who work in a distributed environment are more likely to keep certain information to themselves, even unintentionally, creating some unwanted and unintended secrecy and silos between people and departments. Silos, secrecy, and ambiguity at work decrease motivation, lower employee morale and satisfaction, and hinder collaboration and productivity. This is why building extreme transparency in a hybrid work environment is absolutely essential to develop a successful organization. Building transparency consists of earning people's trust and communicating in an open way. A transparent workplace boosts employee engagement and morale, builds trust between employees, and fosters collaboration. In a hybrid work environment, transparency is achieved through intentional communication and constant feedback, careful listening, and constant adjustment of the communication channels to achieve maximum trust. A shift from the traditional command and control way of doing business to the new bottom-up approach must also take place simultaneously in order to achieve transparency in the organization. Employees no longer want to work for organizations where their voice is not being heard. According to a new survey by ExpenseOnDemand, 64% of millennials believe complete transparency is the most desirable trait of employers.[23]

Luckily, there are different ways for an organization to build transparency in a hybrid work environment, to create the right conditions for a successful team. It all starts with attracting and retaining the right people: transparent people. The people are what makes the culture of an organization, so if the goal is to create a transparent culture, then the focus should be on attracting and retaining transparent people. This can be achieved by paying attention to the hiring process. Candidates should be carefully researched and assessed, and managers should pay more attention to the transparency of the candidate than to their achievements and curriculum. Leaders should also communicate the importance of hiring and retaining transparent employees because they will reinforce the message by doing so. Building a transparent employer brand goes hand in hand with hiring and retaining transparent employees, because a strong, authentic employer brand will act as a magnet for authentic and transparent employees. Organizations should pay particular attention to developing a brand that is transparent and that inspires trust.

Another powerful way for employers to build extreme transparency in a hybrid work setting is to encourage leaders to embrace social media. Many CEOs, including Richard Branson, attribute the success of their organizations to the transparency they built by embracing social media platforms. When CEOs, co-founders and C-suite executives really use social media platforms every day to communicate, they set the tone for transparency and trust, they open a channel for direct dialogue with employees, customers, and members of the public, and they are able to collect unfiltered feedback in real time. This behaviour quickly gets noticed by all employees and customers and becomes proof that the organization truly cares about building trust and transparency with its ecosystem. In a world where face time is becoming less prominent, companies whose leaders communicate frequently and openly on social media rise above their competitors who don't by creating an open dialogue with everyone. Promoting open communication, even outside of social media, is another efficient way to build transparency in a distributed work environment. Ray Dalio and his 'radical transparency' approach to work is a powerful demonstration of how an open communication environment can truly propel an organization to becoming the leader in its category. The chairman and founder of the world's largest hedge fund (Bridgewater Associates) attributes his success to its open communication where everyone, including a new intern, can share their idea openly and change the course of the organization if their idea is regarded as the best one by the rest of the group. The importance of hosting open meetings, prioritizing networking and frequently checking in, as well as creating an open-door policy can truly promote open and honest communication in a distributed work environment.

Promoting open communication is a great way to foster transparency at work and it can be combined with building a flatter organization to achieve even more transparency. While some leaders fear that a flatter organization might be difficult to implement, it is now becoming more important to remove middle management layers in a hybrid work environment in order to build more transparency and to build a more empowering way to work. Organizations like Squarespace are embracing flatter organizations to encourage more collaboration, creativity, and innovation. More importantly, it sends the message that every employee is important, regardless of their job title or status as a remote worker, and it helps all employees feel more connected to one another in a distributed work environment. Building a flatter organization can be achieved by removing unnecessary middle management layers, by empowering front-line employees to get involved with the leadership team, and by delegating decision-making to everyone. Leaders in flatter organizations need to role model more than before to demonstrate how every employee is encouraged to participate in decision-making; leaders should also strive to become more inspirational leaders and lead by consensus in order to build a flatter organization that fosters transparency.

Finally, organizations striving to build extreme transparency in hybrid work should create dedicated employee-to-leadership communication channels. Leading retailers such as Marks & Spencer have embraced this type of employee-to-leadership communication during the Covid-19 pandemic and have created an app where every employee can share their idea directly with their CEO. In a hybrid work environment where teams are more geographically distributed, it can be particularly challenging to create effective employee-to-leadership communication channels; however, there are ways to achieve this, including supporting two-way communication, asking for feedback often and acting upon it, making important company information accessible, encouraging leaders to be authentic, and measuring employee engagement. Regardless of which method you choose to use to build transparency in your organization, it is essential that you consider ways to build trust and transparency in a hybrid work environment because distributed teams require additional support to feel connected and to communicate well. Although you might not be able to implement all of the methods mentioned above, if you start implementing some of them and you become more intentional in regard to building transparency in your organization, you will undoubtedly build the right foundation for a successful team in a hybrid work environment.

Endnotes

1. https://employeebenefits.co.uk/buffer-pay-transparency/

2. https://www.linkedin.com/business/talent/blog/talent-management/what-happened-when-these-companies-made-employee-salaries-public

3. https://bettermarketing.pub/how-buffer-got-229-more-applicants-by-embracing-radical-transparency-f5c30fba293a

4. https://www.businessinsider.com/everyone-at-buffer-can-see-each-others-salaries-2016-1?r=US&IR=T

5. https://zety.com/blog/hr-statistics

6. https://thedailybrit.co.uk/two-thirds-of-millenial-employees-believe-complete-transparency-is-most-desirable-trait-from-employers/

7. https://www.forbes.com/sites/theyec/2020/03/13/how-to-promote-transparency-when-hiring/?sh=55162f8348da

8. https://www.shrm.org/resourcesandtools/tools-and-samples/toolkits/pages/conductingbackgroundinvestigations.aspx

9. https://www.prnewswire.com/news-releases/nearly-three-in-ten-employers-have-caught-a-fake-reference-on-a-job-application-181382901.html

10. https://www.shrm.org/resourcesandtools/hr-topics/talent-acquisition/pages/predictive-assessments-insight-candidates-potential.aspx

11. https://www.workingsolutions.co.uk/blog/social-media-screening-in-recruitment#:~:text= According%20to%20a%202018%20 CareerBuilder,to%20check%20on%20current%20 employees.

12. https://www.inc.com/melanie-curtin/54-percent-of-employers-have-eliminated-a-candidate-based-on-social-media-time-to-clean-up-your-feed-and-tags.html

13. https://www.rightattitudes.com/2008/10/04/7-38-55-rule-personal-communication/

14. https://www.virginmedia.com/corporate/sustainability/goals-and-performance/more-inclusive

15. https://www.inc.com/carmine-gallo/richard-branson-celebrated-virgin-galactics-first-spaceflight-only-way-he-knows-how-its-a-lesson-in-motivating-teams.html

16. https://www.cultureamp.com/blog/open-and-honest-communication

17. https://www.mckinsey.com/business-functions/people-and-organizational-performance/our-insights/reimagining-the-postpandemic-workforce

18. insights/the-organization-blog/fitter-flatter-faster-how-unstructuring-your-organization-can-unlock-massive-value

19. https://www.inc.com/marcel-schwantes/bill-gates-traits-great-leaders.html

20. https://www.sideways6.com/customers/marksandspencer

21. https://www.inc.com/marcel-schwantes/6-companies-that-teach-us-what-it-takes-to-communicate-exceptionally-well.html

22. https://hbr.org/2012/06/leadership-is-a-conversation

23. https://businesschief.eu/human-capital/survey-says-64-millennials-demand-employer-transparency

6 Pillar III: Over-communicate Through All Channels

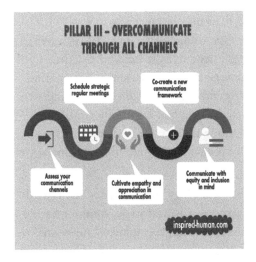

Figure 6.1 Pillar III – Overcommunicate through all channels.

Introduction

When the Covid-19 pandemic suddenly forced organizations to embrace remote work for the first time, the majority of businesses were unprepared for such a sudden shift. For most, it was the first time that employees were no longer working from the office every day, and nothing had prepared them for it. The majority of organizations had no system in place to communicate efficiently to a team that was mostly remote. For legal firm Lenczer Slaght, the timing could not have been better: this is when they launched their brand-new company intranet. From day one, the firm's employees became dependent on the intranet for company updates, news, policies, guides, and more. Lindsey Bombardier, director of marketing and business development, recalls: 'Our immediate adoption rate was close to 100%. I am not sure we would have seen that had we not transitioned to working from home.'[1] The law firm rapidly started using their new intranet as a way to communicate about everything, from Covid-19 resources to Twitter feeds to trusted news to a directory of practice resources helping lawyers, law students, and law clerks find toolkits. Bombardier praised the adoption of the intranet as a game-changer when the firm had to go fully remote on such short notice: 'During the past year, when everything has turned virtual, it's been a saving grace for everyone at the firm.'

Regardless of the technology and approach that is used to communicate in remote or hybrid work, communicating well when teams are distributed geographically is essential to the success of the organization. When employees work in different locations, communication is more challenging. Unconscious bias is more likely to happen because of distance bias, which is the brain's tendency to think people that are physically closer to us are more important than those who are further away. Company culture is also difficult to maintain when employees spend less time together face-to-face. Silos are more likely to happen because of the distance between employees. Maintaining high levels of transparency can also become more difficult when most employees work from different locations.

Overcommunicating is the idea of intentionally repeating a message more than is generally considered necessary. It helps emphasize important messages and reinforces certain key ideas. Overcommunicating brings clarity and removes false assumptions. Since clarity is much needed in a hybrid work environment, overcommunicating simply helps convey key messages. During a time of uncertainty and rapid change, such as the one that most organizations experienced during the Covid-19 pandemic, overcommunicating brings many benefits to the business. In particular, in a remote or hybrid work environment where employees are more separate from each other than in an office setting, the advantages of repeating messages more than usual are significant. Repeating key messages helps avoid confusion. It reduces false assumptions and misunderstandings and brings much needed clarity in the business. Considering that miscommunication or poor communication are often reported by employees as a major reason for not being able to deliver work on time, communication more than usual is especially important in a hybrid work environment. Communicating well in a hybrid work setting also brings purpose. When leaders talk about their company's mission, vision, and goals often, they motivate employees because they remind them of the bigger picture. They help employees see their purpose within the organization, which helps build feelings of belonging and increases employee engagement. Reminding employees about the key goals of the organization or about other important messages also helps build a positive company culture. When leaders are able to bring clarity to the workplace, employees feel more included in the organization, and they feel more comfortable because they can see clearly what matters in the organization. It means that employees are more able to contribute because they better understand what matters and they are more confident about the direction to take. Finally, clear communication creates more accountability. When leaders are able to explain and remind their teams about what is important in the organization, employees have clear direction, and they know what to focus on and to deliver. Clear communication fosters ownership because everyone clearly understands how their role will impact the bottom line.

When teams are distributed geographically and spend little time in an office together, the need for clear communication becomes more important than in a traditional office space setting.

> Leaders of hybrid teams must become chief reminder officers to create clarity, reduce confusion and misunderstandings, provide purpose, build a positive company culture, and develop accountability and ownership.

In order to over-communicate well in a distributed team, leaders and managers need to follow certain steps that can help create the desired cohesion and clarity: they need to assess their communication channels and ensure these are fit for hybrid work, schedule strategic regular meetings, cultivate empathy and appreciation in their communication, create a new communication framework, and communicate with equity and inclusion in mind. Overcommunicating in a hybrid work environment should become part of the leader's routine and should not be seen as a burden but rather as a way to bring the team together. Often, managers and team leaders are afraid to repeat themselves and to sound repetitive to their teams. In reality, people like to be reminded about what matters because they need to know the direction they are supposed to go; according to most surveys on employee communication, the challenge comes from a lack of communication and a lack of clarity, rather than from repetitive communication. Once company leaders and managers understand the importance of building clarity at work, they will no longer fear being perceived by their employees as too repetitive, and they will embrace their roles as chief reminder officers. Following the steps outlined in this chapter will help leaders and managers create clarity for their team in a hybrid work environment, and ultimately build successful hybrid teams who are crystal clear about their purpose, mission, and goals.

In a hybrid work setting, where some employees might work fully remotely, some might work partly remotely and some might work fully in the office, reviewing and assessing communication channels is a very important step to ensure that employees are satisfied with internal communication. Studies have shown that good internal communication improves coordination, boosts employee morale and productivity, and improves efficiency and employee retention. Here are some of the most effective ways that you can measure your communication channels in hybrid work to assess which ones to keep, which ones to lose, and which new channels you should consider adding:

- **Survey employees on your communication channels**
  Consider sending out anonymous pulse surveys to all your employees on a monthly basis, specifically asking them for feedback on internal communication channels. Make sure that you divide employee responses based on those who work full remote, those working partly remote, and those working in the office. Look for some patterns: you might notice that fully remote employees want more team meetings to remain connected, whilst hybrid workers want fewer meetings and more work using shared documents instead, and perhaps office workers want more in-person meetings to promote team building. Consider hosting some qualitative surveys to find out more about the reasons behind certain requests from employees. For instance, you might ask employees in a one-to-one meeting what their preferred communication channel is and what they like about it, and you might also ask them what other communication channel they would like to try that you have not considered before. The important thing is that you pay attention to your employees' feedback on communication because this is your opportunity to significantly improve communication and adjust them to a hybrid work environment, in real time. Remember that your employees' preferences will evolve over time, so it's important to regularly send out communication surveys and adjust accordingly.

- **Assess internal communication engagement**
  Another great way to measure employee engagement with internal communication is to simply track their engagement through analytics. Take time to monitor how your employees are engaging with your various communication channels, including your intranet, your instant messaging app, your internal newsletter, and any other communication channel you may use. Again, compare engagement rates between groups to observe patterns, because remote employees may use certain communication channels more than office workers, for instance. Analyse not only logins but also average time spent in each channel. Try to understand how much employees are really using each channel. Assess email open rates and intranet logins per department and per work group.

Assess Your Communication Channels

Like many other companies who went fully remote during the Covid-19 pandemic, Paddle, a UK-based software company, was forced to re-evaluate its communication channels to ensure it was supporting all employees. Paddle's Chief People Officer David Barker recalls making the decision to go hybrid after a year of remote work: 'At the start of the year, we thought about recalling everyone to the office on a permanent basis. However, since March, we've been asking ourselves, "Why is it so important to have everyone in the office?"'[2] When Paddle surveyed its employees about what their preferred method of work was, it found that the majority of staff wanted flexibility. That's when Paddle realized that team members needed to have the right tools to collaborate well, whether in person, on video, or asynchronously. For Paddle, the transition to hybrid work meant investing in new tools built to support innovation. Bianca Dragan, Paddle's brand and event manager recalls, 'We've used Miro, for example – a virtual whiteboard solution – to brainstorm ideas and capture thoughts and feedback.' The company went even further to maintain playfulness: 'To maintain our company culture, we've also had to become very creative over Slack – we've had Paddlers create custom music videos and we've paid to have Cameos [personalized videos made by celebrities] done for us to celebrate big milestones.' Paddle also implemented meeting-free days as well as a policy in which 30-minute meetings must end at 25 minutes, to give employees a break between meetings. David Barker commented on the need to reassess communication in hybrid work: 'Embracing the way of working we've all been forced into over the past 18 months has forced us to re-evaluate what it means to work. It's been a journey and mindset change, even with our leadership team, but hugely positive for our business. We've honed a great medium where we feel that we can support our people wherever they are, fit around their lives and still achieve our results.'

Assessing your communication channels to make sure that they serve your team well in a hybrid work environment is key to the success of your organization. First, you need to understand and recognize the difference between synchronous and asynchronous communication. Synchronous communication refers to people exchanging information and messages in real and is typical in an office environment. It can be much harder to achieve synchronous communication in a hybrid team because people work in different locations and might not be able to respond immediately to messages. Synchronous communication includes face-to-face conversations and meetings, phone calls, video calls, and instant messages. Although synchronous communication is not always easy to achieve with a hybrid team, there might be situations that require this type of communication, such as:

- When discussing a sensitive topic or sharing feedback.
- When dealing with a sensitive issue that requires immediate attention.
- In emergencies.
- To kick-start a new group project.
- For team-building activities.

On the other hand, asynchronous communication refers to communication that doesn't happen in real time. In this type of communication, there is a lag between the time the message is sent and the time it is received; in remote teams, asynchronous communication is much more prevalent than synchronous communication. Asynchronous communication includes working on a shared document, sending and receiving emails, and using team chat apps.

Regardless of what type of communication you use, it is important that you assess the effectiveness of your communication channels in a hybrid work environment. Good internal communication offers many benefits to the organization including boosting employee morale, engagement and productivity, better operational efficiency, higher employee satisfaction and retention, and better decision-making. Below are a few ways you can assess the effectiveness of your communication channels in a distributed environment:

- **Survey employee engagement**

   One of the most effective ways to assess your internal communication channels is to simply send a monthly pulse survey focusing on communication. Best practice is to make this survey anonymous so that employees feel safe to voice their concerns and ideas in a secure environment. It is also a good idea to analyse results based on the employee working style: the responses from your fully remote employees might differ from those of your fully office-based employees, which might also differ from your hybrid employees' replies. You may notice that fully remote employees prefer one specific communication channel to another, and that your office workers prefer another communication channel. In addition to sending out qualitative surveys, which can be broken down per respondent's type and department, you should also consider hosting focus groups for collecting responses in a one-to-one setting. Taking the time to collect qualitative feedback will help you understand the real challenges and opportunities related to communication in hybrid work. For instance, you might discover that remote workers feel less seen and heard in your monthly all-hands because the attention tends to be on the in-office workers, so you might consider looking for ways to make your remote workers feel more involved in these conversations.

- **Study performance data**

    Most communication tools and technologies offer dashboards that show data related to engagement. Whether this relates to your monthly internal newsletter, your intranet, your instant messaging app, your monthly all-hands Zoom call, or any other internal communication channel, you should be able to export usage data and analyse the results per team. For instance, you can track internal newsletter open rate, click-through rates, and intranet logins. Many companies use an intranet to share company information. You might start by looking at the percentage of employees using the intranet, frequency of intranet usage, peak times around intranet usage, groups and demographics using the intranet more than others, and preferred way to log in (mobile or desktop). If your intranet usage is low, you should consider hosting a dedicated company-wide meeting and ask your employees how they wish to receive and share company information. Using a top-down approach that leaves no room for discussion will stop you from achieving great engagement rates with your communication channels, which will lead to poor internal communication.

- **Pay attention to employee turnover**

    Employee turnover rate may seem irrelevant to internal communication; however, when your organization has outstanding internal communication, employees are more likely to be very engaged and motivated at work and less likely to leave your organization. Pay attention to how many employees are leaving your organization, hold exit interviews, and spend time with the leavers to understand their reasons for departing. According to Trade Press Services, effective internal communications motivate 85% of employees to become more engaged in the workplace.[3] Track your employee turnover rate, in particular based on their working group, as you might notice that fully remote employees are more likely to leave than in-office employees, for example.

If you are looking for some inspiration to create effective internal communication in a hybrid work environment, you might want to emulate some of the most innovative companies that implemented outstanding internal communication strategies. One of these companies is TED, the world-famous non-profit organization spreading ideas via short talks. TED releases talks that have a duration of 10 to 18 minutes maximum. Many studies have shown that the average adult attention span is approximately 15 to 20 minutes, highlighting the need for shorter meetings. Although TED's model is to share interesting ideas in a format that keeps our attention, it is worth considering keeping most of your internal meetings to a 20-minute duration, in order to maintain your employees' full attention. Another company that is well known for its excellent communication is rethinking the traditional approach to internal communication. Virgin and its founder Richard Branson embrace meetings that are held in different spaces. Branson prefers having his meetings in a park or in a cafe, because he believes that new environments help generate new ideas and new perspectives. In a hybrid work environment, you might consider inviting your meeting participants to go for a walk around their local neighbourhood whilst logging in via videoconferencing.

This simple technique could spark more creative discussions and lead to more innovative discussions in your weekly team meetings. Netflix is another interesting example of a company that innovated with their internal communication. At Netflix, communication from management 'comes in the form of short, online memos where questions are answered, essentially making it a living document'.[4] This form of very concise and interactive communication from management makes it more engaging for all employees, whether they are mainly remote workers, office workers, or both.

There are many benefits of assessing your internal communication channels in a hybrid work environment, in particular if hybrid work is new or relatively new to your team. Organizations often skip that step and do not take the time to conduct a communication audit. In reality, running a communication audit is the first step to building the foundation of a successful hybrid organization. First, conducting an internal communication audit provides an opportunity to reflect on what tends to work and what doesn't in terms of sharing information with a distributed team. The audit is a time to reflect and think about what format and channels work better in a hybrid environment. Assessing your internal communication channels will also allow you to set new communication goals for the upcoming year. You might even consider making communication goals part of the business strategy, considering the importance of good communication to run a successful business. Discussing with your leadership team how to incorporate communication goals into their annual targets will help reinforce the focus on effective communication, which is more important than ever before in a hybrid work setting. Assessing your internal communications will help you understand what your employees really think about your organization's communication channels. For instance, if your remote employees make up the largest part of your workforce and they rarely use your intranet and prefer using your Slack channel to receive key company information, you might consider adjusting the way you communicate important company updates moving forward. As mentioned previously, try to understand if certain groups of employees prefer certain communication channels based on their working environment, dividing your employee feedback into remote workers, in-office workers, and hybrid workers, because you might uncover patterns that are specific to each group.

Conducting a communication audit is especially important in a hybrid work setting because it will help you allocate your budget accordingly. By analysing which channels your employees are using, you will be able to notice which communication channels are not being used and you might be able to save on your budget by stopping spending on channels that are not being used. At the same time, you will be able to allocate some of the budget on new communication channels that are more relevant to a hybrid workplace. Remember that the investment you make in new communication channels will fuel the collaboration of your teams and boost your team productivity, so do not worry about spending too much of your budget on internal communication because your distributed teams need to be able to communicate well to work well together. Finally, conducting an audit of your communication channels in a hybrid work environment will help you optimize your existing communication tools. Many organizations that I have worked with had so many different communication tools and apps that most of them were not being fully utilized. Conducting a communication audit will allow you to understand which communication apps are being underutilized due to a lack of awareness. This is a great time to launch your new communication programme to your employees, announcing some exciting changes and sharing how you have used employees' feedback to propose a new communication strategy. You might be able to re-launch some existing communication apps that were not being promoted before and you might run some workshops and lunch-and-learn sessions to showcase these communications tools to ensure that every employee is aware of them and understands how to use them.

> Remember that the adoption of communication tools will only happen when there is a dialogue, so it's important to run regular sessions internally to discuss existing communication channels and adjust accordingly.

When Bosh launched its new employee-focused TED Talk-style format called 'The Spark' in 2017, little did they know that it would become a massive internal communication success. The German multinational engineering and technology company wanted to boost internal communication by offering employees a platform to share their ideas in a new format inspired by the famous TED talks. Employees would share a presentation on a topic of their choice. As a result, each video had an average of 25 000 views internally.[5]

You don't need to launch your own TED Talk–style event or to limit all your meetings to 18 minutes following the TED Talk approach; however, you need to take the time to evaluate your internal communication channels to ensure that they are working effectively for your hybrid team. In a highly distributed team, employees are more disconnected from each other and are less in-the-know of the latest project developments and company updates. It is absolutely essential to review, audit, and measure your communication channels, to ask for employee feedback and to test new ways to communicate internally in order to build the foundations for a successful team. Remember to involve your employees in your decision-making process, especially your fully remote employees, as well as those working partly remotely, so that you get the full picture of what is working for them and what is not. Ultimately, your business will only be successful in hybrid work if every employee feels equally part of the team and part of the conversation, regardless of whether they are fully remote workers, partly remote workers, or office-working employees.

Schedule Strategic Regular Meetings

When Harvard Business School studied the impact of working from home on employees' work habits during the Covid-19 pandemic, the results revealed some significant changes in how meetings were being used.[6] Harvard Business School studied emails and meetings of more than 3 million employees in 16 cities to research the impact of remote working on employees' email and meeting habits. The research team studied team members at 21500 companies in North America, Europe, and the Middle East. When the research looked at meeting invitations, it found that employees in remote work attend 13% more meetings, and the number of people invited to each meeting rose by two, or

14%. The research also revealed that employees sent 5.2% more emails a day and that emails had 2.9% more recipients. The fact that employees are spending more time in meetings when they are no longer sharing an office is not surprising, considering that it is more challenging to keep up with the frequent changes when located in different geographies.

However, keeping up with the latest news and changes is not the only reason why team leaders would pay attention to scheduling key meetings. Recent surveys about the workplace have revealed that the majority of remote employees feel more excluded and isolated from the group than their office colleagues. *Harvard Business Review* surveyed 1153 employees, of which 52% worked from their home office at least some of the time.[7] Those remote employees reported not being treated equally when working from home. Remote workers also reported feeling that their peers mistreated them and left them out, worried that colleagues said bad things behind their backs or made changes to projects without telling them, lobbied against them, or didn't fight for their priorities. When the survey asked remote employees to describe specific skills that great managers had, the responses from over 800 participants included:

- Checking in frequently and consistently
- Using face-to-face or voice-to-voice contact
- Demonstrating exemplary communication skills
- Making expectations explicit
- Being available
- Demonstrating familiarity and comfort with technology
- Prioritizing relationships

Most importantly, nearly half of the remote employees surveyed (46%) said that the most successful managers checked in frequently and regularly with them. Remote workers said that although the frequency of these check-ins varied, they were always consistent and scheduled in their calendar.

What both surveys demonstrate is the importance of scheduling strategic regular meetings with employees in a hybrid work environment. Employees who work in a distributed environment need more frequent check-ins to remain in the know of the latest changes and also to feel included and part of the team. In particular, employees who work fully remotely should have frequent cadence meetings scheduled by their managers to feel like they are part of the group.

Choosing the Right Meeting Cadence

Let's be frank: many employees struggle with the number of meetings in their calendar and sometimes wish they had fewer meetings to attend so that they could focus on getting on with their work. And who can blame employees for feeling this way? Meetings do require some preparation, they take time to attend, they often require some follow-up actions, and not all meetings are productive! So before jumping in and sending out too many meeting invites to your hybrid team, take the time to think about what the right meeting cadence is for you and your team. This will help keep your hybrid team connected without annoying them with unnecessary catch-ups.

A meeting cadence simply means how often you and your team members decide to have recurring meetings. It can be daily, weekly, bi-weekly, monthly, or quarterly. Typically, there are four common types of meeting cadence that each serves a different purpose:

- **Quarterly meetings**
  Quarterly meetings work well for sharing status updates and progress in regard to strategic business goals. They are very relevant for quarterly business reviews that are cross-functional, strategic planning meetings, cross-department all-hands meetings, and performance reviews.

- **Monthly meetings**
  Monthly meetings are great for more meaningful check-ins on strategic topics, allowing employees to share more granular updates on their strategic initiatives. Monthly meetings can be great for skip-level management meetings, which are employees' meetings with their manager's manager, as well as for cross-department management meetings, and department meetings such as 'department monthly all-hands'.

- **Weekly meetings**
  Weekly meetings are a great cadence for deep updates on projects and initiatives within the same team; they are highly recommended for team meetings, including vertical team meetings (regional department) and horizontal team meetings (heads of departments in the same region). Of course, weekly meetings are the best cadence for employees' one-to-one meetings with

their managers, as well as peer meetings for employees from the same department.

- **Daily meetings**

    The most frequent type of meeting, the daily meeting, serves as a daily check-in for high-importance projects or special circumstances projects. As they can be disruptive, they are best used for special occasions. Some teams use daily meetings as part of their agile methodology framework and start each day with a 'daily stand-up'. They are best kept short, focused, and used as a quick check-in channel rather than a problem-solving channel.

The best place to start when choosing the right meeting cadence is to simply ask your team. If you manage a small team, you can ask them in your team meeting or call how often they want to meet. If your team is large, send a survey and get your team members to tell you how often they want to meet.

Remember that you can always change the frequency of your meetings, so even if you don't get it right the first time, you can always revisit the cadence at a later stage. In a hybrid work environment, more frequent meetings are better than less frequent meetings in order to maintain good communication and alignment, as well as inclusion and belonging. A good practice is to ask for feedback often about your meeting cadence; as your team evolves with new people joining and some people leaving, your team's preference might change over time, which is why it is particularly important to collect frequent feedback from your team.

Setting up Cadence Meetings With Direct Reports

Direct reports need special attention in a hybrid work environment. Check-ins with their managers is often their only opportunity to actually get some feedback on how they are doing, understand whether they are going in the right direction, and to check if they are not missing out on something important. Setting up weekly one-to-one meetings with direct reports is really important in order to provide an opportunity for every employee to connect with their direct line manager. Some managers tend to cancel cadence meetings with their direct reports with the excuse that 'something else' came up, and they don't reschedule them.

> Cancelling one-to-one meetings with managers without rescheduling is a sure way to fail at building trust, inclusion, and belonging, especially in a hybrid work setting.

For many employees, their one-to-one meeting with their manager is their only chance to get some real-time feedback on their work; the best managers, as mentioned earlier in the survey by *Harvard Business Review*, are those who regularly check in with their employees. Reclaimai surveyed anonymized aggregated data comparing workweeks between February 2020 and October 2021 across over 15 000 professionals. They found some shocking statistics about the impact of scheduling and rescheduling one-on-one meetings in their 'Reclaimai 2021 Productivity Trends Report'.[8] Their report revealed that more than 40% of one-on-one meetings are rescheduled weekly, taking on average over 10 minutes each to coordinate new meeting times. Interestingly, the report found that on average, 42.4% of one-on-one meetings are rescheduled every week, 118.7 one-on-one meetings are rescheduled per person each year. More interestingly, the research found that on average, 29.6% of one-on-one meetings are cancelled, and professionals with 15 or more meetings every week cancel meetings over 50% more often than the average person, at 127.3 cancelled meetings a year, or 2.5 cancellations a week. With so many one-to-one meetings that are cancelled or rescheduled, it is no wonder that the average remote employee feels more excluded from the group and isolated from the action. Whilst it is important to schedule one-to-one meetings with direct reports in hybrid work, it is even more important to actually attend those meetings.

Setting up Cadence Meetings for Your Team

Teams really come together when they meet. When they are not meeting, teams are actually just a collection of individual contributors working on their individual projects, separated from each other. So setting up a good cadence meeting with your team is very important for the success of your team. Start by paying attention to your current team meeting cadence. Ask yourself if it is serving you and your team as well as it should. As your team evolves and grows in size and complexity, it is possible that the meeting cadence set up some time ago no longer reflects what your team really needs at this time. As always, get direct feedback from your team and ask them how often they want to meet. Consider paying attention to the following factors:

- **Time allocated versus time spent in team meeting**
  The time actually spent in your team meeting might differ from the time allocated to your team meeting. If your regular team meeting often overruns, it is a sign that your team needs more time together. Maybe they need more frequent or longer team meetings. However, if your regular team meeting often ends ahead of time, you should consider shortening the time or even making it less frequent. Discuss the meeting duration with your team members and adjust it accordingly.

- **Team morale**
  Your team's morale and engagement at work is a great indicator of the effectiveness of your team meetings. If most of your team members feel demotivated and disengaged at work, it is a sure sign that your team meetings are not working really well. Your people should feel energized in your meetings and should be enthusiastic and contribute with high energy levels. If that is not the case, you should revisit your team meeting cadence, your meeting format, and agenda. Ask yourself if the people in the meeting are the right meeting participants and if some of them should be in other, separate meetings. Do an audit of your meeting agenda. Ask questions about your team meeting format, cadence, and attendance during one-to-one meetings with your team members to uncover what might be missing.

- **Choosing the right team meeting cadence**
  In a hybrid work environment where meetings are more frequent than in a traditional office setting, it is best to keep meetings as short as possible and to keep

them on track. With Zoom fatigue likely to kick-in more in a distributed work environment, keeping your team meetings minimal will help keep your team members engaged and avoid absenteeism and no-shows. As a rule of thumb, it is best to start with less frequent, shorter team meetings and increase the frequency and duration if necessary, rather than having too many meetings that are too long, because this will lead to employee disengagement altogether. It will also help to set clear expectations and a clear agenda with your team. Add the meeting agenda to your meeting invite for everyone to see. Add a shared document to your team meeting invite where attendees can add questions and notes before the meeting to save time for discussion during the meeting. Finally, always get your team's feedback on your team meeting cadence and always be ready to adjust it accordingly.

As hybrid work is becoming the new way of working for most organizations across the globe, leaders must learn how to communicate well with teams that are more dispersed than ever before. For many leaders, this is a new paradigm and they have never been trained on how to lead and communicate well in a hybrid work environment. Employees who work fully remotely or who work remotely some of the time are reportedly more distracted and more lonely than employees who work full-time from a traditional office. Remote employees and those working remotely some of the time also find it difficult to stay in touch with their colleagues, to be in-the-know and to collaborate well as they struggle to see the bigger picture. Scheduling strategic regular meetings with your teams and attending without cancelling or rescheduling is the best way to communicate well with your hybrid team. From daily stand-ups to weekly team meetings, and from monthly syncs to quarterly business reviews, regular team meetings help teams bond, connect, build trust, communicate on important issues, brainstorm ideas, and share feedback. The secret is to attend these cadence meetings religiously and treat them with the respect they deserve, because as the statistics show, a majority of one-to-one meetings get cancelled and rescheduled. Schedule strategic meetings with your team and attend them, whilst asking for frequent feedback to improve them, and you will be on the right track to building a successful hybrid team.

Cultivate Empathy and Appreciation in Communication

When Covid-19 hit in March 2020, forcing many businesses to close their doors overnight, the hotel industry was hit particularly hard, and hotels were forced to completely change how they operated as businesses. Ewelina Kubaska, HR specialist at Hilton Garden Inn Krakow Airport Hotel, remembers: 'For us, the year 2020 will always remain the symbol of the pandemic and the time of unprecedented changes that we had to adapt to.' Ewelina recalls that like many other hotels, Hilton Garden Inn Krakow Airport had to ask some employees to work remotely for the first time, especially those whose physical presence was not critical. Ewelina shares that her organization changed the working hours and responsibilities of their employees to adapt to the Covid-19 pandemic. As an organization that transitioned to becoming a hybrid team overnight, the Hilton Garden Inn Krakow Airport Hotel quickly realized they had to change the way they communicate with their employees in order to maintain not only communication, but also trust, engagement and team spirit during a challenging time. Ewelina recalls: 'Our board supported us as best they could. We were all regularly informed about the current situation, further plans, and possible scenarios. Our leaders understood that we all needed more empathy and mindfulness, and more attention paid to our feelings and emotions.' As Ewelina shares, 'The leadership style changed – it was now based on communication and compassion. We all listened to each other and motivated each other every day.'[9]

Another company that had to rapidly pivot from office work to remote work during the Covid-19 pandemic is RingCentral.[10] The American cloud-based communications company had to radically change its approach to employee communication in this new fully remote work environment. One of RingCentral's employees explains:

> 'One of the things we found was that as our employees were working remotely, they were working very, very hard. Our productivity went through the roof! But the potential for burnout was real, so we put a number of things in place to both say "thanks" and to protect our people from working all the time. Some examples are a once-a-quarter day off for all employees; weekly virtual activities, from game hour to happy hour – ways for employees to hang out; and more frequent communications from executives to make sure everyone knows where the company is headed.'

RingCentral recognizes that communicating with appreciation in mind can be more challenging in a remote or hybrid environment, so they use video conferencing to connect with all employees to allow some important face time.

Boston-based staffing and recruiting firm Hollister is another business that understood the need to communicate with appreciation in a newly remote work environment.[11] Since March 2020, when the Covid-19 pandemic hit, the staffing company transitioned from office work to remote work. The company is doing a lot to communicate appreciation to all the employees in a remote work environment:

> 'We have a company-wide meeting every Monday morning where our vice president reads acknowledgements that colleagues submitted about each other. We also read two testimonials received from engagement surveys each week to acknowledge our team live. Every employee gets a 'First Cup's on Us' Starbucks gift card and a GrubHub gift card to order coffee and lunch for us on their first day. Every employee also receives an Amazon gift card for both their birthday and their anniversary, along with a personalized anniversary note from leadership and their manager. Further, we host a quarterly company-wide meeting to acknowledge and reward employees across the board, from top sales performers to Unsung Hero, where leadership comments on what contributed to each individual's success and offers a financial reward.'

Communicating with empathy is not just good for employee morale and well-being, it is also great for business.

In 2016, *Harvard Business Review* published the results of a survey on empathy in business which revealed some astonishing findings.[12] The Empath Index is an index that seeks to discover what companies are creating empathetic cultures. The premise is that empathetic workplaces are better at retaining people, attracting and retaining diverse talent, and perform better. The research, run by consulting firm The Empathy Business, breaks down empathy into five categories: ethics, leadership, company culture, brand perception, and public messaging through social media. The survey researched CEO approval ratings from employees, percentage of women on the board, number of accounting and infraction scandals, and employee information from Glassdoor, amongst other metrics. The study focuses on global companies with an emphasis on UK and US companies. The Empathy Index revealed that the top 10 companies in the Global Empathy Index increased in value more than twice as much as the bottom 10 and generated 50% more earnings.

Other research carried out by the leading American analytics and advisory firm Gallup demonstrated that having compassion improves remote worker's performance.[13] In 2018, Gallup released an article sharing the findings of its latest research on the qualities of leaders who inspire performance. The analytics firm surveyed 10 000 people and found that the four qualities best describing leaders who inspire performance are trust, compassion, stability, and hope. In their remote employee engagement survey, Gallup found that employees who agree with the statement, 'My supervisor, or someone at work, seems to care about me as a person,' are more likely to:

- Experiment with new ideas.
- Be advocates for their employer.
- Support co-workers personally and professionally.
- Feel equipped to strike a balance between their work and personal lives.

Gallup's research found that leaders who want to show they care about their remote workers should do the following:

- **Give recognition and praise often**
  According to Gallup, employees want to do a good job, and they want their manager to notice their good work. Remote employees are not physically present to receive thank yous, so words of appreciation, texts, and emails are great ways to prove that you notice and appreciate their work.

- **Ask for their opinions**
  Gallup also found that a great way for managers to show their compassion to remote workers is to ask them for their opinion. The consulting firm recommends that managers ask their remote employees what they think or what they would recommend given a particular situation.

Although it seems like common sense to communicate with particular empathy and compassion in a remote or hybrid work environment, my observations from having worked with dozens of organizations is that this is simply not the reality in many organizations. First, the vast majority of team leaders and managers have never been trained or educated on how to attract and retain talent in a hybrid work environment. This lack of education and awareness translates into a total absence of empathy and compassion for their hybrid and remote employees. Second, most team leaders are so busy focusing on their day-to-day work, fighting fires, and responding to business emergencies that they forget to check in with their people, let alone taking the time to ask their remote and hybrid employees how they are doing. Finally, some managers simply believe it is not their job to care for their people or to build trust, as they view it as something that has nothing to do with the business. For all of these reasons and probably more, the majority of team leaders and managers do not proactively communicate with empathy and compassion, and this is especially damaging in a hybrid work environment where most employees feel more disconnected and isolated than in-office workers. Communicating with empathy and compassion builds psychological safety, which is when employees are able to show up, speak up, and contribute without any fear of negative consequences, mockery, or criticism. Being particularly empathetic and compassionate builds trust and rapport, which sets the foundation for a productive, enjoyable, and even fun work environment. Empathy is really the secret ingredient to building a successful team, particularly in a distributed team, where each employee might have very different challenges, needs, access to information and knowledge, and even different cultural backgrounds if teams are geographically distributed across different countries, continents, and time zones.

In order to cultivate empathy and appreciation in communication, hybrid work managers can follow a few strategies that will significantly boost their team morale and productivity. Even though some team leaders and managers may never have led with empathy and appreciation before, they can learn and practise empathetic communication by following a few simple techniques and becoming role models for their hybrid teams:

- **Acknowledging and complimenting employees' work**
  Remote workers and even hybrid workers can often feel that their hard work is not being recognized as much as their office-based counterparts. For those

working most of the time 'out of sight' at home, it is easy to feel forgotten and left out from the office 'high fives' and spontaneous cheers.

Managers who practise complimenting their employees' work are showing they care about their people. In particular, team leaders who praise their remote and hybrid employees as much as they praise their office-based people build a culture of empathy.

Complimenting and praising contributions makes people feel good about their efforts, encouraging them to work better and setting the tone for the type of communication that is expected and valued: empathy and appreciation-based communication. People working in such an environment where praising is common practice are more likely to praise their co-workers' work, which in turn, creates a virtuous cycle of praise, appreciation, and empathy. Managers can also show their appreciation of their hybrid team by offering rewards. These rewards can be financial such as additional payment at the end of the month, or they can be non-financial such as extra days of annual leave. The important thing is that managers demonstrate they care about their hybrid workforce by giving them a reward or praise, because all employees will feel they are being recognized, valued, and appreciated by their manager, whether they are 'out-of-sight' remote workers, or partly 'out-of-sight' hybrid employees.

- **Asking for feedback**
  A study of 1100 employees, published by *Harvard Business Review,* found that remote workers

feel more left out.[14] According to that study, nearly half of the respondents said that most successful managers checked in frequently and regularly with remote employees. Respondents also reported that the most successful managers are good listeners and inquire about workload and progress. The research demonstrates the importance of asking for feedback when managing a remote team or even a hybrid team. Asking for feedback should not be limited to just work, workload, and progress, it should also be about work–life balance, any need or help, or anything else that the employee feels is important. In addition, great managers take time to build trust and rapport with each of their employees before asking for feedback.

Hybrid and remote workers will only share feedback openly if they feel safe enough to do so. Team leaders and managers should prioritize building rapport with their people every day by practising checking in often, asking open questions, and practising active listening.

Asking for feedback and building trust takes some extra time, but the rewards are infinite because it will boost employee morale and engagement, productivity and retention, and collaboration and communication. In addition, managers can leverage technology to collect feedback by sending monthly employee pulse surveys to gather quantitative feedback. However, in order to get the full picture of what their hybrid employees really need, team leaders should ask for feedback during their one-to-one meetings with their direct reports.

- **Supporting flexible work**

    Even though hybrid teams most likely are allowed to work in a flexible environment, managers of hybrid teams should pay attention to how they support flexible work for their employees. During my many years of consulting companies and even working with companies who support flexible work, I have observed that the company policy about flexible work is not always translated into practice by all managers. An article published by *The Atlantic* titled 'What Bosses Really Think of Remote Workers' revealed that people who work from home get fewer raises and promotions.[15] The reality is that many employees fear that embracing hybrid and remote work will hurt their careers and they fear repercussions on their promotions, pay rises, and opportunities for growth due to hidden bias towards office workers. Managers who truly want to build a successful hybrid team by communication with empathy should become vocal advocates of flexible work. Be sure to talk about your support for flexible work during your team meetings, your one-to-one check-ins, and any company all-hands meetings. Remember to ask your team members how they feel about their current working environment and listen to their requests. Find out if any of your team members are going through a challenging time who might need special working arrangements.

    Team leaders who actively promote a flexible work environment with their team members show they care about their people and actively support their remote and hybrid employees so that everyone can work from their preferred location and can juggle any other commitments. Such managers demonstrate empathy and nurture a culture of camaraderie and support, which is fundamental in a hybrid workplace.

The transition from traditional office work to hybrid work has changed communication forever. In particular, when many employees had to become remote workers overnight during the Covid-19 pandemic, their needs and expectations related to communication shifted as they expected more empathy and more appreciation. A SWNS research study of 2000 Americans, conducted by OnePoll on behalf of Motivosity, found that remote workers are not feeling the love from managers, with half of employed respondents working from home saying they have not felt much gratitude from their job since they stopped commuting.[16] Cultivating empathy and appreciation in communication is an important strategy to build, nurture, and retain teams in a hybrid work environment. Managers who practice empathy and appreciation with their hybrid employees build the foundation for a successful hybrid team by setting the tone and becoming role models.

Co-create a New Communication Framework

When Amy Edmonson, professor of leadership at Harvard Business School and specialist in organizational behaviour was asked what the future of work will hold, especially regarding remote and hybrid models, her answer was: 'The most successful teams will write the playbook together.' Edmonson recommends evolving workplace communication by breaking old habits and developing a new method of workplace communication. She describes this as a 'linguistic system of science, that co-opts our communicative habits with parts of the scientific method, creating a culture that says: here is what I see, here's some hypotheses and experiments that we could try. Let's remain open to the data we receive and others' ideas'.[17]

One company that has embraced the co-creation of a new communication framework in hybrid work is Ernst & Young. EY has created a Design Council to navigate the shift to hybrid work and ensure that all employees are being represented. EY put together a team of employees from different functions, regions, and levels of seniority, selected on their ability to act as change champions at all levels of the organization. Together, the team is using their diverse perspectives to create EY's 'Way of Working' guidance. IBM also adopted a similar approach when it hosted a 'Think Forward Jam': the company hosted a two-day virtual event for more than 34 000 employees to co-create guidance, foster accountability, and share best practices and recommendations regarding how to work together in a hybrid work environment.[18]

Co-creating a communication framework is creating a basic structure of communication by working with all employees. It is a two-way, open dialogue between the organization's leaders and its employees, where all parties engage in a discussion to jointly define a solution of communication that works for everyone. The benefits of co-creating a communication framework with employees are significant and justify this approach. First, leaders who co-create the communication framework with their employees gain access to more creative thinking and expertize. Individual contributors in your team bring a wealth of perspectives to the discussion that you would not get from consulting with only your leadership team. Your employees are also experts in their own fields, and they understand better than anyone else what communication works for them and their team members. They also are directly impacted by the communication channels and therefore their contribution to the communication framework will directly improve communication. Second, co-creating a communication framework with employees taps into a community that is extremely willing to help. Think about co-creation like a more democratic way to create new policies. Co-creating improves collaboration and gives a voice to all individual contributors, fostering unity and open discussions. Finally, co-creating a communication framework improves employee experience. It says to your employees that you care about what they want, and it makes your team feel valued, heard, and seen. It allows organizations to transform their employees into fans and advocates. Regardless of what drives your organization to co-create a communication framework with your employees, the simple process of opening the discussion to all employees will open access to greater creativity and expertize, give you access to an engaging community willing to help, and transform your employees into advocates.

- **Identify and articulate new engagement rules**
  One of the first steps of co-creating a new communication strategy for your hybrid work team is to identify and articulate new engagement rules. In a hybrid work setting, communication is more asynchronous than in an office setting, employee distractions from work are more frequent (family members, kids, pets, deliveries, etc.), and it is more challenging to achieve a sense of familiarity between

employees organically. Rules of engagement regarding communication and collaboration must be discussed and adjusted according to the new paradigm and based on your team's preferences. For example, your team might decide to host either meetings that are fully in-person or fully virtual, excluding meetings where some participants are in the office and some are joining virtually, if they feel it offers a more equal opportunity to speak to all participants. Your team might also decide to record and share all video conferences and share notes from each meeting for every employee to see, making information more accessible to everyone inside the organization. Some companies have also decided to make all employees' emails accessible to all employees inside the organization, to increase transparency and knowledge sharing. Team leaders and managers should ask their own teams how they want to engage with each other, what channels they prefer to use for each project and how they want to share information in a way that is productive and mindful of everyone's work preferences. Some teams might prefer to use instant collaboration tools for project collaboration such as Slack, whilst others might prefer to share using shared documents on Google drives, and other teams might prefer to communicate over emails.

Do not assume that your own personal preferences are the same as your team members, and ask your team how and when they want to collaborate.

Once you have identified how your team likes to collaborate, make sure that you write down these rules of engagement, share them with the wider organization, and make them accessible to everyone. You should also revisit these rules regularly as new members join your team and as new needs and trends arise, to refresh them and keep them current.

- **Document processes and technology**
  Documenting processes and technology is often skipped over and regarded as tedious by many leaders. Most of the teams I have worked with didn't have documented processes and technology related to communication. However, writing down processes can significantly improve collaboration, especially for new starters who are not familiar with the systems and the people. A 2007 study from the Wynhurst Group found that newly hired employees are 58% more likely to still be at the company three years later if they had completed a structured onboarding process.[19]

  Discuss with your team members what they would like to document in relation to communication guidelines. Write a handbook for your team on how to communicate in a hybrid work setting and share this handbook with your new starters and the wider organization.

> Documenting communication processes and tools reduces risks of misunderstandings and miscommunication, allows everyone to spot possible problems in communication and act on them, helps identify roles and responsibilities to the wider team, and empowers people to be accountable and proactive with their communication.

- **Organize office working days**

    Although the trend for remote work and hybrid work is growing globally, the need for face-to-face meetings remains strong to build camaraderie, rapport, trust, and belonging. According to a Hubspot study, 95% of people agree that better business relationships are built through face-to-face meetings.[20] According to a *Forbes* study, 84% of executives say they prefer in-person meetings for their ability to build stronger and more meaningful business relationships.[21] Many other studies report that face-to-face meetings allow teams to build more meaningful business relationships, facilitate communication, allow people to bond, and improve team building. In a hybrid team, managers should discuss with their team members the importance of organizing face-to-face meetings regularly to build rapport and improve communication. Allow your employees to decide how often they want to meet in person, where they want to meet in person and what format they prefer for a face-to-face gathering. Ask your team members what works for them and how you can facilitate in-person meetings. Invite all your employees to contribute to the discussion and listen to what is being said. Once you have heard from all your employees, write down the takeaway and book some dates in everyone's calendars for in-person meetings. By involving your people in organizing those in-person office working days, you build a more participative approach to communication in your team.

- **Schedule time for frequent improvements**

    One of the key success factors for your communication framework is its adoption by your team members. If your employees do not follow the communication guidelines, it is a signal that your guidelines need adjusting. In a survey by Really Simple System on CRM adoption, which surveyed 500 users of CRM software in the United Kingdom, it was revealed that 83% of senior executives said getting the staff to use the software was their biggest challenge.[22] And it is not just technology adoption that can be a challenge: if employees do not adopt the communication channels recommended in the communication guidelines, the entire communication will suffer, and the team will not be able to collaborate efficiently. Discuss with your team members how often you should revisit your communication framework. Ask your employees when they would like to refresh the team's communication guidelines and tools to adjust to their changing needs. Remember to frequently check in with your employees on the communication guidelines and find out if anything needs to be changed.

The process of co-creating a communication framework can be achieved through design thinking. This methodology is a powerful way to co-create a solution with your employees. Design thinking is a human-centred approach to innovation that takes into account the needs of people, the possibilities of technology, and the requirements for business success. Design thinking means working together to look for opportunities and focus on problem solving. It always starts with people and needs, and it involves understanding and listening, establishing a culture of trust and openness. The design thinking process is structured around five key steps:

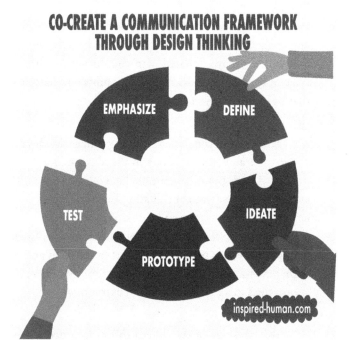

Figure 6.2   Co-create a communication framework through design thinking.

- **Empathize**
    The first step in design thinking is to empathize and discover. Listen to your employees and ask them to share what a good communication framework would look like in a hybrid work environment. Find out about your team's challenges related to communicating in a distributed environment. Try and listen with an open mind, and be open to all the challenges you might hear about.

- **Define**

    This step is about stating your employees needs and challenges. Define the key issues and challenges that your employees shared with you during the first stage of empathizing. Identify pain points and patterns that need to be solved.

- **Ideate**

    This step of the design thinking process is where you involve all your employees in the idea creation process. At this point, you are challenging assumptions and creating new ways of thinking. Encourage your employees to be creative and think of new ways to communicate well in a hybrid work environment. Invite your employees to present their ideas to the team and to share new ways they think communication should be approached in a distributed work environment.

- **Prototype**

    At this stage of the design thinking process, you and your employees start creating solutions together. You and your employees will develop several communication frameworks for your hybrid team based on the ideas from the previous stage. Make sure that you create more than one communication handbook so that you keep your options open.

- **Test**

    Try your new communication guidelines with your team. As you experiment and test your new communication framework with your hybrid team, you might revise and adjust it based on your team's feedback. Keep testing and experimenting with your new communication framework until your team is happy with it and adopts it fully.

In March 2021, Citigroup announced its move to a hybrid working environment. Jane Fraser, CEO of Citigroup, shared that the decision to embrace hybrid work was due to the many benefits that employees received from the flexibility of working from home. However, Fraser also explained that 'the likelihood of employees adopting a hybrid work model depends on how well they can collaborate with co-workers and management from their home office'.[23] Fraser also announced a ban on video meetings on Fridays, introducing 'Zoom-free Fridays', and announced that a percentage of Citigroup employees would continue to work fully remotely. In Citigroup's case, it is clear that a new communication framework needs to be created in order to enable the best possible collaboration between employees and management. The CEO herself pointed out that only employees and teams who are capable of collaborating well in hybrid work will be able to continue to work in a hybrid setting. The importance of co-creating a new communication framework cannot be underestimated in that context.

Taking the time to understand how to communicate as a team is a fundamental step. The key is to involve everyone in the decision-making process and to ask every team member to share how they prefer to communicate, what channels they want to use, and what type of communication works best for them.

Hybrid work is a new reality for most managers, teams, and organizations globally. The vast majority of employees, team leaders, and managers have never been trained on how to communicate in a distributed work environment.

Ultimately, the success of your hybrid team will depend on how well your distributed team is able to collaborate in a distributed environment, so take the time to co-create a new communication framework that your employees will embrace and adopt.

Communicate With Equity and Inclusion in Mind

Hybrid work offers many benefits to employees because of the flexibility it provides and the choice people have when it comes to where they work. For many employees, having the option to work remotely at least some of the time is about the ability to work at all. Making office work mandatory simply excludes many qualified people from jobs they are capable of and willing to perform. Employees with family care responsibilities rely on remote work and hybrid work. The majority of carers for young families are women. Women, many of whom are mothers, have expressed a stronger desire to continue working remotely than men.[24] Employees with physical disabilities also rely on remote and hybrid work: commuting creates a significant obstacle to many disabled people and working from the office can be a major roadblock for individuals with mobility limitations. Employees living in remote locations due to lower income, far from city centres where most offices are located, need remote and hybrid work options because many struggle to commute to office locations. Employees with lower income simply cannot afford to live near office locations, which often excludes them from job opportunities. Remote and hybrid work gives people with lower income access to work, which they would not be able to do otherwise. However, as inclusive as hybrid work is compared to the traditional office work setting, it can also cause some inequalities and exclusion for the remote and hybrid workforce.

Remote and hybrid employees are more likely to experience distance bias, which is when 'out-of-sight' colleagues become 'out-of-mind' for managers and leaders. Distance bias is when employees or managers unintentionally favour employees who are closest to them (in the office) over those who are further away (working from home).

Although often unintentional, like most biases, it is very real. A research study of more than 1000 employees in the UK by Censuswide revealed that a third of workers believe that being in the office is ultimately better for career progression, and 39% are convinced that working from home may hurt their career.[25] Proximity bias is our tendency to prefer those who are closer to us in space and time. Yet for UK-based occupational psychologist Ali Shalfrooshan, 'prioritization of safety doesn't always lead to accurate judgements'. Shalfrooshan explains: 'We all can reflect on occasions where the people we sit near are the people we know the best and feel the most kinship to.'[26] Research from the Office for National Statistics (ONS) revealed that between 2013 and 2020, people who worked from home were on average 38% less likely to have received a bonus compared to those who never worked from home. Similarly, the analysis showed that, between 2012 and 2017, people who mainly worked from home were less than half as likely to be promoted than other workers and were less likely to receive training.[27] The problem caused by hybrid work is that it could create an unintentional two-tier workforce: one workforce made up of in-office employees who get the credit, promotions, trainings, career advancement opportunities, glamour work, and mentoring, and another workforce made up of remote and hybrid workers who get forgotten, excluded from career advancement opportunities, who are not getting rewarded and promoted for their work, and who get denied mentoring and glamour work. Although this two-tier workforce might not be the result of intentional exclusion or discrimination towards remote or hybrid workers, it is as damaging as intentional discrimination for those hard-working, high-performing hybrid and remote employees. Organizations must learn how to communicate with equity and inclusion in mind in order to create a fair and equitable hybrid workplace where all employees are developed and retained.

In September 2021, the US Equal Employment Opportunity Commission (EEOC) found that ISS Facility Services Inc., a facility management firm, unlawfully discriminated against an employee who asked to continue working remotely due to health conditions and fired her for it. Ronisha Moncrief, a health and safety manager for ISS Facility Services, requested accommodation to work from home two days a week as an accommodation for her chronic obstructive lung disease and hypertension. Shortly after her request, ISS placed its staff on modified work schedules where employees worked from home four days per week due to the Covid-19 pandemic. However, in June

2020, ISS required all staff to return to in-person work at its facility five days per week. When the facility reopened, Moncrief requested accommodation to work remotely two days per week due to her pulmonary condition that caused her to have difficulty breathing and placed her at a greater risk of contracting Covid-19. The company denied Moncrief's request and, shortly thereafter, fired her.[28] This case illustrates the risks of creating an inequitable work environment for remote and hybrid workers, who are more at risk of being penalized in their career because of their choice of working fully or partly remotely. Not all remote and hybrid employees risk being fired for doing so, but they most likely risk missing out on promotions, career advancement opportunities, rewards and recognition, mentoring opportunities, pay rises, and more. What's more, the inequalities in the workplace persist and have even been accentuated during the Covid-19 pandemic.

According to the World Economic Forum, closing the global gender gap has increased by a generation from 99.5 years to 135.6 years during the Covid-19 pandemic, as per its Global Gender Gap Report 2021.

The report pointed out:
'On one hand, the proportion of women among skilled professionals continues to increase, as does progress towards wage equality, albeit at a slower pace. On the other hand, overall income disparities are still only part-way towards being bridged and there is a persistent lack of women in leadership positions, with women representing just 27% of all manager positions.'

The World Economic Forum's 2021 Gender Gap Report also revealed that there has been a decline of women's hiring into leadership roles, creating a reversal of 1 to 2 years of progress across multiple industries. Other studies, such as McKinsey's 'Women in the Workplace' report, have also reported that men are promoted at a 30% higher rate than women. According to the US Bureau of Labor Statistics, men have earned more than women since 1979, the first year with available data. And according to the US Census Bureau '2019 American Community Survey', Black and Hispanic women face the biggest pay gap when comparing earnings to non-Hispanic white men.

With all the pre-existing inequalities in the workplace between men and women, white employees and non-white employees, and all other inequalities, the hybrid workplace needs to foster an inclusive and equitable workplace for all its employees. In a post-Covid workplace, where workplace inequalities are more top of mind than ever before, employers must implement strategies to communicate with equity and inclusion in mind to attract, nurture, and retain diverse talent in a hybrid environment. Here are four strategies that you can use to communicate with equity and inclusion in a hybrid work environment:

- **Overcommunicate**
  In a hybrid work environment, full-time remote employees and employees who work remotely part-time can feel more excluded than their office peers. Managers must make an intentional effort to overcommunicate with all employees in order to make everyone feel included and part of the team. Replicating office informal interactions is a great

way to overcommunicate with everyone. Remote workers tend to work with less supervision, so managers may be less aware of their workload or accomplishments.

When managers over communicate via video calls, emails, phone calls, group meetings, or one-to-one meetings, they are able to replicate the informal interactions that take place in the office, and they make remote employees feel more connected; managers are also able to stay informed of their remote employees' contributions.

Communicating more frequently also helps create more inclusion. Sending weekly emails to your team, hosting informal chats with remote employees, encouraging pre- and post-meeting socializing, holding company-wide meetings to sync up and highlight your team's success internally help to improve feelings of inclusion amongst your hybrid team. Refreshing your internal communication channels also helps create more inclusion and equity between remote employees and office employees. Describe explicitly which channels should be used for various types of communications (email, chat apps, meetings, etc.), encourage more inclusive practices such as choosing to use group email threads where project discussions are visible to everyone rather than one-to-one emails, ensure that your one-to-one meetings structure allows sufficient time for feedback from each employee about their work setting, and document conversations via digital channels rather than in person.

- **Ensure equitable practices**

    In a highly distributed team, there is a higher risk of favouritism towards employees that are office-based versus remote employees. Distance bias and proximity bias are at play, and they tend to make team leaders unconsciously prefer office workers who are closer to them over remote workers who are further away. Start by reviewing your workplace practices. Traditional policies no longer work in a hybrid setting. Standard performance reviews and evaluations might hold hidden bias towards in-person workers, giving them an unfair advantage.

> Managers should focus on results-based performance rather than office-presence evaluations to ensure that remote workers are assessed fairly.

Be intentionally transparent. A big part of people's perception of fairness comes from transparency. Be open about the principles you are using to determine who gets promoted, who gets recognition, who gets new projects, who gets new assignments, etc. Share the experiments you are considering for new work methodologies with everyone in your team. Communicate about business necessities and the ways you will need people to make unique contributions toward a shared purpose. Hold people accountable. When you take action to address bad or unfair behaviour or a lack of results, you contribute to a more equitable culture. This is especially true in hybrid work where remote and hybrid employees pay extra attention to their manager's behaviour and use it as a basis for what is acceptable and what is not. When people feel others are doing their jobs, delivering results, receiving appropriate recognition, and being held accountable, it goes a long way toward creating a culture where a sense of fairness is pervasive.

- **Monitor feedback closely**

    Rethinking your approach with a strategy of fairness and equality in mind is key to communicating with inclusion and equity. Take concrete steps to ensure equal treatment of remote workers. Recognizing the needs of remote workers can be a challenge, so managers should monitor qualitative feedback of remote workers closely. By talking openly with your team, acknowledging the issues that hybrid work can bring, and hosting team meetings to discuss hybrid work, you can create a hybrid workplace that is fair and equitable for all employees. Companies without obvious metrics for measuring feedback on employee inclusion may need to create new assessment methods; consider sending employee engagement surveys with a focus on hybrid work. These employee inclusion assessments address many forms of bias including preferential treatment on the basis of presenteeism, race, gender, and sexual orientation, among others.

- **Organize team-building activities**

    When the Covid-19 pandemic hit in 2020, almost 26% of workers had a different employer that same year, meaning that some employees have never interacted with their new teammates in person before. Organize a group walk 'n' talk. If your team is tired of staring at a screen, then head outside! For those in the office, get together and go for a walk while you hold a meeting. For those working remotely, encourage them to call in and take a stroll during the discussion. Have those working remotely share where they're walking and what they're seeing. Or make it a competition by having your team track their steps and see who can get the most steps! Start a unique conversation. Making small talk via videoconference has its limitations. Build a numbered list of unique questions, have each team member choose a number, and ask them the corresponding question. You can choose from work-oriented questions like: *What's a department you'd love to learn more about, and why?* Or take a more personal route and ask questions like: *What was your favourite holiday destination, and would you revisit that location?*

Communicating with inclusion in a hybrid work environment means that every employee feels heard, valued and seen, and is able to take part in the same activities and enjoy the same experiences, regardless of their work setting. It means that all employees are treated fairly and respectfully, have equal access to opportunities and resources, and can contribute equally to their team's success. It means that different perspectives are always heard and valued and that all employees contribute equally to projects. In order to create a truly inclusive and equitable workplace in a hybrid team, managers and team leaders must be intentional in their communication. Overcommunicating, replicating office informal interactions, ensuring equitable practices, monitoring feedback closely and organizing team-building activities will help create a more inclusive team and ensure that remote and hybrid employees are truly included and feel like they belong to the team as much as in-office employees.

Conclusion

In a hybrid work environment, the 'out-of-sight, out-of-mind' adage can unfortunately become true. As many remote employees have reported in various surveys, working remotely, even part-time, can make people feel excluded, isolated, less aware of the latest developments, and even miss out on career advancement opportunities. The most successful hybrid teams are those that are able to overcommunicate through all channels to make every employee part of the conversation, regardless of whether they work from the office five days a week or whether they never work in the office. A lot of companies used the Covid-19 pandemic as an opportunity to completely revisit their internal communication; from adopting new communication technologies and tools, to changing the way they interact with employees. From adopting a new intranet technology like legal firm Lenczer Slaght, to re-evaluating communication channels like UK-based software company Paddle, to embracing a new leadership style based on communication and compassion like Hilton-many companies have pivoted and changed the way they communicate with their employees during the Covid-19 pandemic. However, the common theme amongst all these companies is that they all started communicating more, and more often, when they transitioned to a hybrid work environment. Whether it was by adopting a new communication technology like legal firm Lenczer Slaght, to facilitate better internal communication, or whether it was by embracing a new communication style based on better communication and compassion like Hilton, most organizations that transitioned to hybrid work embraced communicating more and better.

A new work environment requires new communication channels. First, you need to understand and recognize the difference between synchronous and asynchronous communication. Synchronous communication refers to people exchanging information and messages in real time. Asynchronous communication refers to communication that doesn't happen in real time. Assess the effectiveness of both types of communication with your hybrid team and identify which works best for each scenario. Survey employee engagement and analyse results based on employee working style: the responses from remote employees may differ from those of office-based employees. You may notice that fully remote employees prefer one specific communication channel to another, and that your office workers also prefer another communication channel. Study performance data to find out what tools are actually being used and what tools are not being adopted by your hybrid team. Monitor the performance of your monthly internal newsletter, intranet, instant messaging app, monthly all-hands Zoom call, or any other internal communication channel. Pay close attention to your employee turnover; when your organization has outstanding internal communication, your employees are more likely to be very engaged and motivated at work and less likely to leave your organization. Monitor how many employees are leaving your organization, hold exit interviews, and spend time with your employees leaving to understand their reasons for departing. Track your employee turnover rate, particularly based on their working group, as you might notice that fully remote employees are more likely to leave than in-office employees, for example.

Scheduling strategic regular meetings is also key to communicating well in a hybrid work setting. *Harvard*

Business Review found that remote employees think great managers arrange frequent and consistent check-ins, and they reported that this is the top skill of a great manager, together with using face-to-face or voice-to-voice contact, demonstrating exemplary communication skills, making expectations explicit, and being available. Choosing the right meeting cadence will help achieve a balanced communication flow. Whether it's a quarterly meeting, a monthly meeting, a weekly meeting, or even a daily stand-up, you must implement a meeting cadence and ask your team what works best for them. Setting up cadence meetings with direct reports and team members is also fundamental, especially in a remote work environment, because direct reports need special attention in a remote work environment. Setting up weekly one-to-one meetings with direct reports is really important in order to provide an opportunity for every employee to connect with their direct line manager. Some managers tend to cancel cadence meetings with their direct reports with the excuse that 'something else' came up; however, cancelling one-to-one meetings without rescheduling is a sure way to fail at building trust. Research found that more than 40% of one-on-one meetings are rescheduled weekly, taking on average over 10 minutes each to coordinate new meeting times. Don't become a statistic attend all your cadence meetings.

Cultivating empathy and appreciation in communication is a key element of creating a successful hybrid team. Research found that companies with empathetic leadership generate more value and produce 50% more earnings than those with no empathetic leadership. Another research by Gallup found that

compassion at work improves remote workers'
performance. Ensure that you intentionally communicate
with empathy by acknowledging and complimenting
employees' work, asking for feedback and truly supporting
flexible work.

Co-creating a new communication framework with
your team will also help build the foundation for a
successful hybrid team. Identify and articulate new
engagement rules with your team members, document
processes and technology, organize office working days, and
schedule time for frequent improvements. Involving
everyone in the decision-making process and asking every
team member to share how they prefer to communicate will
help you create the right communication framework for
your hybrid team.

Communicate with equity and inclusion in mind.
Communicating with a focus on inclusion in a hybrid work
environment means that every employee feels heard and
valued. In order to create an inclusive hybrid workplace,
managers must be intentional in their communication.
Overcommunicating, replicating informal office
interactions, ensuring equitable practices, monitoring
feedback closely, and organizing team-building activities
will help create a more inclusive team and ensure that
remote employees are truly included and feel like they
belong to the team as much as in-office employees.
Communicating more frequently, through the right
channels, with the right meeting cadence, in an inclusive
and collaborative way, will set up the foundation for a
successful hybrid team. As Henry Ford famously said: 'If
everyone is moving forward together, then success takes care
of itself.'

Endnotes

1. https://www.thoughtfarmer.com/blog/5-organizations-mastering-the-hybrid-workplace/
2. https://www.bbc.com/worklife/article/20210915-how-companies-around-the-world-are-shifting-the-way-they-work
3. https://www.hrcloud.com/blog/8-employee-engagement-statistics-you-need-to-know-in-2021#f
4. https://blog.circleloop.com/companies-with-great-internal-communications
5. https://staffbase.com/blog/internal-communication-examples/
6. https://hbswk.hbs.edu/item/you-re-right-you-are-working-longer-and-attending-more-meetings
7. https://hbr.org/2017/11/a-study-of-1100-employees-found-that-remote-workers-feel-shunned-and-left-out
8. https://reclaim.ai/blog/productivity-report-one-on-one-meetings
9. https://humanpanel.com/empathy-in-leadership/
10. https://www.comparably.com/news/how-7-companies-celebrate-their-employees-remotely/
11. Ibid.
12. https://hbr.org/2016/12/the-most-and-least-empathetic-companies-2016
13. https://www.gallup.com/workplace/236210/having-compassion-enhances-remote-workers-performance.aspx

14. https://hbr.org/2017/11/a-study-of-
1100-employees-found-that-remote-workers-feel-
shunned-and-left-out

15. https://www.theatlantic.com/politics/archive/2021/05/
can-working-remotely-hurt-your-career/618922/

16. https://www.forbes.com/sites/
bryanrobinson/2020/11/16/new-research-says-
remote-workers-want-more-appreciation-from-their-
leaders-or-else/?sh=db1b13d5fa2c

17. https://digiday.com/marketing/
breaking-old-habits-hybrid-working-setups-call-
for-different-ways-of-communicating/

18. https://www.greatplacetowork.com/resources/blog/
successful-hybrid-work-models-have-these-5-
things-in-common

19. https://www.shrm.org/resourcesandtools/hr-topics/
talent-acquisition/pages/onboarding-key-retaining-
engaging-talent.aspx

20. https://techjury.net/blog/networking-statistics/
#gref

21. https://www.wework.com/ideas/professional-
development/creativity-culture/benefits-of-in-person-
meetings#:~:text=According%20to%20a%20
Forbes%20survey,and%20more%20meaningful%20
business%20relationships.&text=Face%2Dto%2Df
ace%20meetings%20cement,social%20bonds%20
and%20strengthen%20relationships.

22. https://blog.tmcnet.com/telecom-crm/2007/11/30/
crm-adoption-biggest-problem-in-83-percent-of-cases-
wigan-gets-crm-tre.asp

23. https://www.compt.io/hr-articles/companies-doing-a-hybrid-work-model

24. https://hrexecutive.com/why-hr-needs-to-stop-the-clock-on-the-womens-recession/?eml=20210403&oly_enc_id=6577B4185945G7Z

25. https://www.businessinsider.com/bosses-worry-proximity-bias-hurt-remote-employees-career-progression-2021-11?r=US&IR=T#:~:text=Another%20study%20of%20more%20than,home%20may%20hurt%20their%20career.

26. https://www.bbc.com/worklife/article/20210804-hybrid-work-how-proximity-bias-can-lead-to-favouritism

27. https://www.peoplemanagement.co.uk/news/articles/home-workers-less-likely-promoted-or-receive-bonuses-ons-stats-reveal#gref

28. https://www.fisherphillips.com/news-insights/eeoc-files-first-remote-work-discrimination-lawsuit.html

7 Pillar IV: Unify Cross-Cultural Hybrid Teams Through Cultural Awareness

Introduction

When Meera Sapra joined the Indian multinational technology company Zoho, working remotely out of New Delhi, she quickly discovered that working 2184 km away from the main headquarters in Chennai and with colleagues in the USA in different time zones meant she had to evolve and adapt to make it work.[1] Not only was Meera working with teams across different time zones, but she was also working with people from different continents and different

Figure 7.1   Pillar IV – Unify cross-cultural hybrid teams through cultural awareness.

countries. Meera noted, 'What could get in the way though, are cultural differences.' She observed that it can be challenging for people from different cultures and languages to work together, especially if they are not physically in the same location.

Meera also explained that for many Asian countries that are high-context cultures, 'communication is about maintaining harmony and not causing offence'. Many Asian people may be unable to say, 'I don't understand this', or 'I cannot do this', or 'I would need more time to do this'.

For example, Meera shared that the great Indian head bobble (head-shaking gesture) could mean any of these:
'Good'
'I understand'
'Yes'
'No'
'The answer is no but I just don't want to say it.'
Her American colleagues would not necessarily understand these on a video conference call!

Meera pointed out that her way to prevent miscommunication due to cultural differences was to follow up with chat messages summarizing the action items. Meera also shared that after many interactions with her colleagues from South India, she was able to get over the stereotype of 'all South Indians are introverts' that persists in India.

Cross-cultural hybrid teams are made of people from different national backgrounds, native languages, and cultures who have a flexible work structure where some people work remotely and some work in an office. In a business environment, companies must make sure that their employees work together effectively, even when people have very different cultural backgrounds, upbringing, and social norms. Employees need to learn subtle differences in communication in order to work well together.

Renowned American anthropologist Edward Twitchell Hall developed the concepts of high and low context cultures; he explained:

In high-context cultures like China, when a manager assigns a task to subordinates and asks if they can complete it, the employee is more likely to say 'yes' even when they don't understand or if they know that they can't complete the task. It can feel too uncomfortable to say 'no' even

> High-context communication relies more heavily on shared context and so the message is often implicit, which is true in China, India, and many Asian countries; low-context communication is more explicit as it relies more on the words used and less on a shared context and the relationship between the speakers, which is the case in the USA and most of Europe.

though that's what they really mean. Likewise, if a Chinese employee says 'yes' and agrees with the positive feedback they receive at work, they may be perceived as arrogant and will not leave a good impression on other Chinese colleagues. American author and professor at INSEAD Business School Erin Meyer points out that when conflicts and misunderstandings happen in cross-cultural teams, they are often caused by different cultural attitudes toward authority and towards decision-making. Meyer explains that Japanese people, for example, are hierarchical in their views toward authority, and they defer to the boss and wait for instructions rather than take the initiative.

However, even if cross-cultural hybrid teams can cause some challenges due to cultural differences in communication and due to asynchronous communication, they also present many benefits to the organization. Multicultural teams have more empathy, respect, and understanding for their colleagues and customers. This is because people themselves come from a different cultural background, so they understand first-hand the need to be more empathetic with someone whose native language is not English and whose cultural background is not the one where the company is headquartered. Cross-cultural teams are also more respectful to employees and customers from different backgrounds because of their own lived experiences, which have shown them that different cultures have different norms and values.

Multicultural teams are also much more creative than teams comprising people from the same cultural background. This is because each person in the cross-cultural team looks at a problem from a very different perspective, which brings creative thinking to the team and ultimately more innovation. Each team member looks at a problem through their own lens and perspective, which comes from their distinct cultural background. This enriches discussions and offers new and different perspectives to business challenges.

Multicultural teams are also polyglot by nature, and they open up new avenues to market the company products and services. Having team members speak different languages brings local knowledge of different customer segments, which is a valuable resource to sell and market products and services. This allows the company to reach new markets, to deliver a better customer service and better customer experience, and to provide better customer support to new regions.

Multicultural teams also solve problems faster and better than homogeneous teams. Many studies have demonstrated that very diverse teams were able to solve problems faster and with fewer mistakes because they are more prepared to discuss, being used to working with different cultures, and they make fewer mistakes due to the extra preparation they bring to the table. Ultimately, cross-cultural teams generate more revenue from innovation.

In a global economy, where hybrid cross-cultural teams have become the norm, it has become more important than ever to learn how to develop effective communication and collaboration for multicultural teams working in a virtual environment. The following sections will explore how to unify cross cultural hybrid teams through cultural awareness so that team members can work effectively together. Managers play a key role in setting the foundations of a successful cross-cultural hybrid team and they need to learn and implement the fundamental principles of building and retaining a successful multicultural team in a virtual environment.

Promote Psychological Safety and Inclusion

In February 2016, a research paper was published by five academic researchers from Bar Ilan University, the University of California, Carnegie Mellon University, and Israel Institute of Technology, titled 'Psychological Safety and Collective Intelligence in Multicultural Globally Dispersed Teams'.[2] The study examined what multicultural teams that are geographically dispersed need to do to work effectively despite all the challenges. The study found that 'teams' effective performance depends on interaction between two factors: psychological safety and collective intelligence'. The study observed three independent samples of MBA students, located at different business schools (USA, Europe, Asia, and the Middle East). The participants were randomly assigned to culturally diverse and globally dispersed virtual teams to work on a proposal for establishing a new business in a foreign country.[3] The research found that team members' global identity facilitates team psychological safety, and consequently, team performance. It found that information sharing enables the effect of team members' global identity on psychological safety; it also found that socio-emotional content sharing in the kick-off meeting (specifically self-disclosure) has a positive impact on establishing psychological safety.

Outside of academic research, university-led studies, and laboratory analysis, real-life businesses have also discovered the incredible benefits of psychological safety to build a successful team. One of the most successful businesses in the world, Google, conducted a two-year study on its employees to find out what makes a great team. After two years of conducting over 200 interviews with employees, analysing more than 250 attributes, and observing 180+ teams, Google identified what makes teams successful. Google found that psychological safety was by far the most important dynamic of a successful team. Google found that employees on teams with higher psychological safety were less likely to leave the organization, more likely to harness the power of diverse ideas from their co-workers, generate more revenue, and are rated as effective twice as often by executives.[4]

Psychological safety appears to be the secret to unifying teams and making them work better together. So what exactly is psychological safety? And what does a team with psychological safety look like? According to William A. Kahn, psychological safety is being able to show and employ oneself without fear of negative consequences of self-image, status, or career. William A. Kahn is professor of organizational behaviour at Boston University's Questrom

According to American scholar of leadership, teaming, and organizational learning Amy Edmondson, psychological safety is 'a belief that one will not be punished or humiliated for speaking up with ideas, questions, concerns, or mistakes'. Edmondson also describes team psychological safety as a shared belief held by members of a team that the team is safe for interpersonal risk taking.

Author Timothy R. Clark has identified four stages of psychological safety:
1 – included
2 – safe to learn
3 – safe to contribute
4 – safe to challenge the status quo

School of Business and is often regarded as the father of employee engagement.

Edmondson adds: 'It describes a team climate characterized by interpersonal trust and mutual respect in which people are comfortable being themselves'. Teams that are psychologically safe can easily admit that they have made a mistake. Team members have no shame sharing failures, errors, and mistakes with their peers because they know it will not be used against them. Team members acknowledge that they don't have to know everything. In psychologically safe teams, employees know that they might not understand everything, and they can ask basic questions; they understand that it is acceptable to have some gaps. Employees in psychologically safe teams value everyone's opinions and inputs equally.

Employees are empowered to speak up, share their ideas, and contribute to the conversations equally, regardless of their seniority level in the organization.

In a multicultural team where team members come from different countries and cultures (and time zones), it can be especially challenging to create psychological safety due to the cultural differences and styles of communication. Israeli employees and Dutch employees are more comfortable with giving direct negative feedback in front of a group and they regard this as normal communication. Chinese and Indian employees prioritize group harmony and show respect to their managers, and therefore, would not usually speak up in groups where their manager is present or would not challenge a decision even if they disagree. Many cultures in Western countries usually refrain from providing negative feedback for fear of hurting someone's feelings, a concept that author Kim Scott defines as 'Ruinous Empathy.' Scott explains that Ruinous Empathy is 'nice but ultimately unhelpful or even damaging. It's what happens when you care about someone personally but fail to challenge them directly.' Speaking up, contributing to the decisions and conversations, and challenging the status quo can be challenging for employees from countries and cultures where it is not widely accepted to do so, especially in the presence of a group of people and with someone in a position of authority such as a manager or team leader.

So it's important to establish a few guidelines for international hybrid teams so that they can benefit from a culture of psychological safety and team members can speak up safely together. Below are some strategies that you can use to promote psychological safety in your international hybrid team:

- **Set the tone and lead the way**

In a virtual-first work environment, employees look up to their team leader, managers, and leadership team more than in a traditional office setting for direction on how to behave. Leaders, managers, and team leaders set the tone and demonstrate in action what behaviours are acceptable, how to communicate with one another, and what the standard of collaboration is.

Leaders hold a position of power, influence, and authority. What they communicate, how they communicate, and who they communicate with get picked up even more in a hybrid work environment, especially when teams are more global. Over the years of consulting with organizations, I have noticed that when leaders set the tone and embody the behaviours that they preach, their teams tend to perform better than the rest, and this is especially true in a highly distributed, highly international team. Some of the key attributes and behaviours of these leaders include being vulnerable and modelling that it is acceptable to make mistakes, frequently asking people for their thoughts (this includes asking all the people in their team, not the same people all the time), publicly saying thank you to people sharing opinions, and using a direct and respectful style of communication. In addition, some of the most successful leaders also challenge assumptions, commit fully once decisions are made, and respond positively to challenges.

One of the organizations I was consulting had recently appointed a new vice president of sales, based in London, to lead their international team in Europe and Asia. When he joined, he quickly noticed that the international team meetings were dominated by the European team and the Asian team remained quiet. He started asking people in the Asian team for their opinion frequently, by calling people out and asking what they thought. He listened, took notes, and always made a point to thank them for their contributions. Over a period of time, he even changed the date and time of the international team meeting, so it worked better for the team in Asia and also changed the format and agenda to accommodate requests from the team in Asia. Gradually, he noticed that the team in Asia started contributing more and sharing ideas without being prompted. When leaders proactively ask employees to share their thoughts (especially those from cultures traditionally more hierarchical) and thanking employees for their contributions, they set the tone for what kind of communication is expected and promote psychological safety, especially in a highly international and distributed team.

- **Share positive examples**

    At first, team members may struggle with the idea of speaking up often, saying they don't understand something, or even challenging the status quo. This is especially true if the team is very international, and some team members come from cultures where preserving the harmony of the group is seen as the most important element of working together. In a hybrid work environment, managers have to be very intentional about creating psychological safety, and sharing positive examples will help.

Sharing examples of successful organizations that have achieved amazing success based on their focus on psychological safety will help convince your team that they should try it.

Talk about Google's Project Aristotle and explain how Google teams who had the most psychological safety performed the best. Explain that when Google employees have a safe space to take risks and make mistakes without fear or repercussions, they become the most productive teams in the organization. Share that the reason why Google named its project 'Aristotle' is because of the philosopher's famous quotation: 'The whole is greater than the sum of its parts.' Talk about how Amazon's top leadership focuses on creating psychological safety to be successful. Amazon founder Jeff Bezos was personally responsible for this, as his office name plate famously said, 'Tell me even more candidly'.[5] The more examples you can share of successful companies adopting psychological safety as their modus operandi, the more you will convince all your team members to adopt this way of working together.

- **Help people connect**

  If your team is mostly working remotely and rarely meets in person, chances are that team members have not had many opportunities to build rapport. Building rapport and camaraderie can be especially challenging if team members are in different countries, working in different time zones. However, in order to build psychological safety in a team, there must be a foundation of trust which is built on knowing each other.

As Patrick Lencioni says in his best-selling book *The Five Dysfunctions of a Team*, an absence of trust is the first sign of a dysfunctional team, because it leads to a fear of conflict, a lack of commitment, an avoidance of accountability, and an inattention to result. Lencioni suggests that highly functional teams have a lot of trust as a solid foundation.

Managers should focus on helping their team members connect with each other and build rapport. Team leaders should facilitate conversations that are focused on building connections, rapport, and camaraderie between team members. Host a meeting to discuss everyone's hobbies, favourite holiday destinations, and interests outside of work. Create a Slack channel for your team to discuss personal news and hobbies, start an Employee Resource Group about common interests in your team, and ask people if they want to join a book club about their favourite topics. Creating a space for your team members to share their personal interests will help your people connect and create more psychological safety in your hybrid team.

Creating a psychologically safe work environment is like building a house of cards; it takes a long time and a lot of effort to build it, but the smallest wrong move can destroy it and make you have to start all over again.

• **Be vigilant and watch out for harmful comments**

This is especially true in a virtual work environment where it takes longer to build trust and distance makes it harder

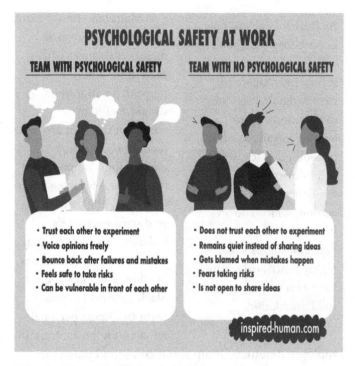

Figure 7.2 Psychological safety at work.

to build rapport. Being a manager in a hybrid team is a
balancing act, but the rewards of building a psychologically
safe team are significant. Managers should pay extra
attention to seemingly harmless comments from team
members such as 'You should already know this, we already
talked about it last week', 'You should be familiar with that
process since you have been here six months', 'She made a
mistake and that's why we did not succeed at that project,
it's her fault', or 'We already discussed that and decided what
to do, so there is no need to debate it anymore'.

These apparently innocent comments set the tone that not knowing something or asking questions is not well received, and it creates a fear of speaking up and a fear-based culture where people are more likely to remain quiet, not share ideas, and not challenge decisions for fear of being criticized for doing so. Team leaders, managers, and the leadership team should push back on harmful comments such as, 'Everybody knows this!' and 'You should remember that because we talked about it already', and instead, they should emphasize that we always welcome all types of questions and comments because that's how we grow as a team.

Figure 7.3   Harmful comments to watch out for.

Promoting psychological safety and inclusion in a highly international, highly distributed team can be challenging, but it has its rewards. It helps create a speak-up culture where everyone feels safe enough to share their ideas, bring creative solutions to the table, and it fosters innovation.

Managers who set the tone and lead the way, share positive examples, help their people connect and remain vigilant, and watch out for hurtful comments, are able to encourage a psychologically safe work environment where every employee feels truly included and safe enough to be part of the conversation, regardless of their culture, location, or job title.

Create a Cross-Cultural Awareness Programme

N. Radhakrishnan, Industry Consultant in Global Business Services at IBM based in India, had been working hard to close a contract from a Dutch client, with not much success. The Dutch prospect had a choice of four vendors at the time, and IBM was just one of them. N. Radhakrishnan had attended IBM's training programme on understanding cultural differences, and he had learnt that the Dutch enjoy waterfront views because it reminds them of their home country. So when his prospect sent a team from the Netherlands to India, he took the opportunity to invite them to a waterfront restaurant for dinner. N. Radhakrishnan did get the contract, due to his choice of the waterfront restaurant.[6]

Hamsanandhi Seshan, Director of Communications and Global Delivery at IBM, was on a flight to Germany when he read up on German cultural traits. He found out that Germans are 'culturally more inclined to risk taking' and she shared that with them. However, she learnt that they have a very linear method of thinking, and she thinks more in a random manner herself.[7] Technology giant IBM is well-known for offering training programmes to its employees about cultural norms of nations, including one which is called 'country navigator'. The programme tells IBM employees if certain nations are more task- versus relationship-oriented, if the country's communication is more direct or indirect, etc. IBM's cross-cultural awareness programme helps workers to find out about the cultural characteristics of the country they will be working with and to find out how they match up with their own cultural characteristics, which facilitates better communication and collaboration.

But it's not only the technology giants of this world who understand the importance of cross-cultural awareness programmes; airplane manufacturer Boeing also embraces initiatives to raise awareness about cultural diversity. Boeing uses 'GlobeSmart', which is an online resource for employees to learn about cultural norms of countries they will be working with. Boeing hosts cultural talks in a 'lunch and learn' format as well as diversity summits two times a year. Boeing's executives can also take part in a programme called 'passport series' to learn about cultural diversity.[8]

Cross-cultural awareness programmes, also called cross-cultural training, is a practice aimed at increasing people's understanding of other cultures and improving their ability to deal with people from different cultures so that

Cross-cultural awareness programmes help employees increase their cultural awareness and become more sensitive to their co-workers' cultural backgrounds so that they are more respectful of cultural differences and more inclusive in their communication styles.

they can perform well in a highly diverse cultural environment.

Ultimately, they help employees in highly multicultural teams to work better together. A famous quote perfectly explains what cross-cultural awareness does: 'If you do not intentionally include, you unintentionally exclude.' A lack of cross-cultural awareness leads to unintentional hurts and microaggressions, unconscious bias, favouritism, and acts of exclusion towards people who are from a different background.

Cross-cultural awareness programmes add many powerful benefits to international teams, especially those working in a hybrid environment where opportunities to spend time together are rare. One surprising benefit is that employees actually learn about themselves. They become aware, sometimes for the first time, of their own cultural norms, which they may have taken for granted and now understand are linked to their own cultural background. This helps employees become more open to working with people from a different culture than their own, through exposure to their own culture norms. Cultural training also builds team trust and confidence because when people are exposed to different cultures as a team, they are better equipped to have conversations together. These types of awareness programmes also help reduce hidden bias and stereotypes that employees may hold because they shed light on the different norms that exist within each culture and help employees realize some of their own unconscious biases. These awareness programmes help teams become more open to new ideas and perspectives, which in turn helps them become more innovative. Employees suddenly realize that other perspectives and points of view exist outside of their own, and they become more open to new approaches. In addition, teams that join cross-cultural awareness programmes improve their listening and interpersonal skills because they become more sensitive to other people's backgrounds and they become more aware of differences, which creates more interest in other cultures and naturally makes them more likely to listen. Finally, cultural diversity training helps everyone really focus on what they have in common rather than what they don't share, because it helps employees realize that they actually share a common desire to succeed as a team, a common desire to learn and grow together, and to communicate well.

In a hybrid work environment, cross-cultural awareness programmes should be managed with particular attention because there are fewer informal opportunities for employees to meet and build rapport. Here are some effective strategies that you can use to create a cross-cultural awareness programme in your international, hybrid team:

- **Plan for success**

  Before you start implementing any cross-cultural awareness programme, pause and consider how much your team is already going through. Chances are that your team is already trying to navigate how to work well together in a hybrid work environment, what communication channels to use, where to share all the information, and how to communicate well despite the time zone differences. If you approach your team members with another new programme to embrace, they might just push back and not buy into it due to other conflicting priorities. What's more, many studies have shown that mandatory training doesn't work as effectively as optional training, because when people feel they have no choice, they are not emotionally attached to it. On the other hand, when training is made optional to attend, those who actually join it feel much more emotionally invested in it because they made a choice to attend and, as a result, they are more likely to embrace it and be committed to it. In other words, find a way to get your team excited about a cross-cultural awareness programme so that they are interested, and they fully embrace it.

A great way to do this is to ask your team what they would like to learn about each other's cultures. You can make it fun and ask your team to choose what they want to focus on. The important thing is to let them guide you so that they feel involved in this programme. Make sure to also 'sell' it to them; share examples of successful teams that have embraced cultural diversity awareness and have become twice as productive as a result. Show your team studies and research papers about teams with a high level of cultural awareness and how this has made their innovation and performance better. Explain why you believe that cultural awareness in your team will help everyone better understand each other and communicate in a hybrid work environment. Consider leveraging existing channels and regular meetings to facilitate this cultural awareness programme. For instance, if you already have a weekly team meeting every Monday, consider using that time to invite a keynote speaker to talk about cultural awareness; or if you already have a Slack channel about diversity and inclusion, leverage it to discuss cultural awareness training. If your team has a weekly newsletter, use that to discuss the benefits of cross-cultural awareness programmes. Whatever channel you use to communicate about it, leverage existing communication channels to get maximum exposure and avoid spamming your busy team.

Sharing an anecdote also helps increase employee engagement, because people respond to people and get inspired by other people they can connect with. Encourage your employees to share their stories related to cultural awareness without forcing them to do so. Volunteer yourself to share a personal anecdote when you said something that reflected on your cultural background, and you realized that you didn't take into consideration your audience's cultural background.

• **Use storytelling**

Telling stories is a powerful way to communicate about values and beliefs because stories are universal, and they transcend cultures and individual backgrounds. Stories also engage people because they connect with emotions.

Tell a tale of a team that you knew that used to celebrate cultural holidays and as a result unified its team members. Many education programmes use storytelling as a tool to connect learners with new material. Research by

Northeastern University in Boston that studied the effect of
story on our attention span revealed that participants who
were given more story elements in their scenarios generated
more brainwave activity than those who received bare-fact
scenarios. This activity reflected their heightened attention
to the task.[9] Stories have the capacity to capture our
attention in ways that simple fact sharing and data sharing
don't. Think about the last time you got lost in a movie at
the cinema; your capacity to connect with the story allowed
you to be fully engaged in the experience, much more so
than if you had been reading a research paper with facts and
figures. Stories are also much easier to remember than data.
Listening to a story can teach us a valuable lesson and can
make us take action. When we hear stories with a bad
outcome, we are more likely to take action to avoid that
outcome. Ultimately, stories are powerful tools to make us
change our mind and our behaviour. If you are committed
to changing your team's understanding of cultural
differences, consider telling stories, asking your team
members to share stories, and inviting great storytellers such
as keynote speakers to talk about cultural awareness.
Leveraging storytelling as a tool to increase cultural
awareness in your team is a powerful way to create a
successful cross-cultural awareness programme in a highly
distributed team.

- **Prioritize culturally aware communication**
  If your time is limited and you have to limit the
  scope of your cultural awareness programme, prioritize
  cultural awareness in communication. Good
  communication is at the core of a unified team, so
  make sure that each of your team members truly
  understand what it means to communicate with

awareness of the cultural differences that exist in your team. At a very basic level, culturally aware communication is when one understands that the person they are interacting with may come from a different cultural background where communication norms wildly differ from their own. Language barriers may cause a non-native English speaker to misunderstand informal ways of saying things, expressions, or inside jokes. For example, when I worked with an American software vendor whose teams were often scattered across the US, the UK, and the rest of Europe, the European team, whose English was their second language, often didn't understand certain expressions used by their American counterparts, which led to misunderstandings, delays in responding, and frustrations on the part of all parties. By simply becoming more aware of these local colloquialisms and expressions, the US team replaced these informal ways of speaking with more standards ways of speaking and the communication significantly improved.

Raise awareness about differences in communication styles. For instance, many cultures in Asia prioritize harmony and hierarchy over individualism and sharing the best ideas. This can translate into team members not speaking up when someone senior is in the same meeting or keeping quiet when asked to challenge a decision or share their ideas. On the other hand, certain cultures such as those in the Netherlands or in Israel have a very direct communication style, where employees will share feedback directly, including negative feedback, even in front of a group. If employees from these two very different cultures are in the same team, and if they are not aware of the cultural differences, it may translate into misunderstandings, frustrations, and even an inability to work together. If you focus on raising awareness about differences in cultural tones and communication styles, you will empower your team members to understand cultural differences in communication styles so they can adjust accordingly.

- **Understanding that learning is a journey**

     As human beings, we all have unconscious biases, and we all communicate differently based on the culture we were raised in. A key step in creating an efficient cross-cultural awareness programme is to set the expectations with your team members that understanding cultural differences is a journey, not a destination. If you are truly able to articulate that practising and learning about understanding cultural differences is more important than being perfect, you will set your team up for success. Most people do not engage in cultural awareness programmes for fear of saying or doing the wrong thing. By setting the tone that we are all in this together and you are all here to learn, you will attract more interest and get more engagement from your team members.

> Remember that starting a cultural awareness programme is already in itself a significant step towards cultural awareness, because most organizations don't have one and many teams either ignore it completely or are paralysed by the fear of getting it wrong. Starting a cultural awareness training programme is already half the battle won.

Implementing cross-cultural awareness training is a key step in unifying international hybrid teams because it helps people learn about themselves and become more trusting of each other, builds confidence, reduces unconscious bias, and opens up new perspectives. By planning for success and leveraging existing communication channels such as team meetings and newsletters, leveraging storytelling to connect with your team and drive change, prioritizing culturally aware communication such as language barriers and communication style differences, and by understanding that learning is a journey and not a destination, you will be able to embrace cross cultural awareness programmes and set your international team up for success, despite time zone differences and cultural differences.

Consider Language Fluency and National Communication Norms

US tech giant Google has long been known for its success as an organization, which is largely due to its strong organizational culture. A big part of the company culture is based on sharing positive employee feedback. Google's performance review form asks managers to list all the things employees did really well. Once this has been done, Google asks managers to 'list one thing this person could do to have a bigger impact'. When the US tech giant opened its first offices in France, it was confronted with the French culture of giving feedback, which focuses a lot more on criticism and a lot less on praise! A French manager recalls, 'The first time I used the Google form to give a performance review, I was confused. Where was the section to talk about problem areas?' What did this employee do *really* well? The positive wording sounded over the top. The French Manager at Google recollects, 'After five years at Google France, I can tell you we are now a group of French people who give negative feedback in a very un-French way.'[10]

French cosmetics brand L'Oréal also learnt about international communication challenges when it expanded in other countries. Open debates and differences of opinions have always been an important part of the company culture. One L'Oréal manager shared, 'At L'Oréal we believe the more we debate openly and the more strongly we disagree in meetings, the closer we get to excellence, the more we generate creativity, and the more we reduce risk.'[11] However, in some cultures, this communication style clashes directly with the preferences for group harmony. A Mexican employee commented: 'In Mexican culture, open disagreement is considered rude, disrespectful, and too aggressive.' Another employee from Indonesia explained: 'To an Indonesian person, confrontation in a group setting is extremely negative, because it makes the other person lose face. So it's something that we try strongly to avoid in any open manner.'[12]

One British technology company I consulted with shared with me a story of a cultural misunderstanding with a Dutch employee. The Dutch employee had joined the UK company a few months ago and had delivered a presentation to her manager, who was British. The manager had said that the presentation was 'fine', so the Dutch employee was pleased with the feedback she received and went on with her day. When she learnt that her manager had been complaining about her presentation to other colleagues, she could not possibly understand why, since she heard her manager say that her presentation was fine. When we sat down to discuss the situation, we uncovered that this was due to cultural differences. The Dutch are typically open and very direct when giving feedback, including negative feedback. However, the British are much more subtle and focus on being polite when giving feedback, and much of the communication happens implicitly - people need to 'read between the lines' to understand what is actually being communicated.

Another US software vendor that I consulted with was struggling with communication with their Chinese office. The US company, which was headquartered in Jersey City, near New York City, had opened offices in China to help with software development, design, and back-office activities. However, the marketing team based in the US and in Europe started complaining about the design team in China. One marketing manager in the US complained that 'the Chinese designers are not creative at all, they keep asking for more information about the design brief and they don't make any decisions by themselves, which keeps delaying our projects and we are always late!' On the other hand, the Chinese designers claimed that 'the US marketing team never gives enough direction regarding the project, they don't give clear guidelines so we don't know what is expected of us'. What happened is that the US culture is based on individual contribution, innovation, and equality; whereas in Chinese culture, hierarchy is very important and individual contributors expect to receive step-by-step instructions about their task. In addition, English was the second language of the Chinese team and, as a result, their lack of fluency in English sometimes resulted in some miscommunication and misunderstandings.

National communication norms, also known as cultural norms or social norms, are sets of unwritten and implicit rules of behaviour and attitudes based on shared beliefs from a specific group, country, or region. These rules are often unspoken so they can be difficult to acknowledge and to understand for someone who is not part of the group, country, or region. These unspoken guidelines set the tone for what is appropriate and what is inappropriate behaviour, especially when it comes to interactions.

National communication norms can have a big impact on how a business operates with international teams who work virtually, because they can differ widely from country to country. Teams that take the time to learn and understand different cultural norms are more likely to succeed in business as they improve their communication internally and externally.

Language fluency or language proficiency is the ability of a person to use language with a level of accuracy to understand and speak it like a native speaker. One can be called 'fluent' in a language when they can confidently and accurately express themselves in a language. In business, language fluency is vital in creating good communication, and employees whose native language is not English may sometimes struggle to understand some expressions in English language, second degree concepts, idioms, inside jokes, and other implicit messages when native English speakers interact with them. Common English idioms such as 'ice breaker', 'crying over spilled milk', 'a dime a dozen', 'spilling the beans', 'beating around the bush', 'taking a rain check', or 'wrapping your head around' might confuse non-native English speakers and might block the communication if they are too shy to ask what the meaning of this idiom is.

There are many incredible benefits to intercultural awareness in an organization. Cultural awareness helps people understand their own culture and understand how to adjust their communication style according to their counterpart's culture. For example, if someone comes from a country where direct feedback is the norm and they interact with someone whose culture prioritizes group harmony, they will be able to adjust their communication style accordingly. Cultural awareness in a very international team helps build rapport because everyone becomes more aware of their colleagues' cultural backgrounds and becomes more understanding. As a result, there is more trust in the team and more psychological safety, meaning that employees feel safe to speak up and share their ideas without fear of being judged or criticized. Cultural awareness also helps teams become more successful in dealing with prospects, clients, and vendors because they are more sensitive to their cultural backgrounds and are more able to adjust their communication style with them to achieve better business relationships. Finally, cultural awareness training helps reduce implicit bias and stereotypes, which helps improve relationships, communication, and collaboration in the long term.

So how do you pay attention to language fluency and national communication norms in a hybrid team? Below are a few simple strategies that you can use to consider language

proficiency and cultural communication norms in a highly
distributed team:

- **Consider language training for your team**

  Language training may not sound like something
  that your team needs at first sight; however, if your team
  is international with many employees living in different
  countries and different continents, chances are that some
  of your employees might not understand all the idioms,
  expressions, and ways of saying things that are used by
  your native English speakers. Language training can
  improve understanding on the part of all the non-native
  English speakers in your team, and can help boost
  employee confidence, especially if they are not used to
  speaking English in a business environment. Perhaps
  they have learnt English at school and have used it
  scarcely, and now they don't feel confident using it at
  work. According to the software company Rosetta Stone,
  70% of business users surveyed said that language
  training has made them more confident.[13] Language
  training also helps non-native English speakers be more
  productive and perform better because they can better
  communicate with their English-speaking colleagues.
  Among employees who participated in company-
  sponsored language training, 71% say their job
  performance has improved as a result.[14] Language
  training also helps non-native English speakers feel more
  engaged at work because they are better able to feel part
  of the conversation and part of the team as a result of
  feeling more confident speaking English.

- **Use simple language and repeat yourself**

  As the manager or team leader of an international
  team, your role is to set the tone for what behaviour is

expected in your team, especially in a hybrid team environment where employees look up to their manager to understand what behaviour is expected of them. When you use simple language to express yourself at work, and you repeat yourself often, you establish the rule implicitly and other team members are more likely to do so as well.

Avoid using jargon, idioms, or complicated vocabulary when it's not necessary. Simplicity in language is key, especially when your team is hybrid, international, and distributed over different countries.

Instead of saying, 'the ball is in your court', say 'it is now up to you to make a decision or take the next move'. Instead of saying: 'I am sitting on the fence', say 'I am not sure what to do'. Instead of saying 'it is a no-brainer', say 'it is really obvious'. In your emails and in your team presentations, pay attention to the language you use and prioritize language and words that are straightforward and uncomplicated. Many business presentations are complex and use jargon, abbreviations, and technical language that is often unnecessary and confusing. Choosing simple language will help convey your message better in an international team. You might also consider using visuals that are universally understood in your presentations. These can include infographics, charts, pictures, or any other visual that conveys your message in an easy way. Do not be afraid to repeat yourself. In a hybrid team, sharing information via multiple channels can make it overwhelming and drown important information in noise; when people repeat themselves often, they ensure that their message will reach its audience better. This is especially true in a very international team, whose native language might not be English and who might struggle to understand what you are communicating. Remember that the best leaders are really 'chief reminder officers' because they understand the importance of reminding their team of what is really important.

- **Discuss cultural differences and show respect**

> Simply talking about different cultural norms as a team can go a long way in educating your people about them.

One of the technology companies that I consulted for had a Monday morning weekly call with the entire region to start the week, and the tradition was that whoever was presenting that day had to start the conversation by discussing an interesting fact about the country they came from. Sometimes the host would talk about a famous cultural holiday in their country and the meaning behind it, sometimes the host would talk about a tradition typical in their country, or even talk about a typical way to greet people in their country. The rest of the team really enjoyed these stories because it educated them about different norms and traditions that their colleagues were used to. As a result, that team reported better communication, increased productivity, and created a better rapport over a period of time. Another company that I worked with used to celebrate all the national holidays of the countries that their employees came from! They celebrated Bastille Day on July 14th in honour of their French employees, they celebrated Guy Fawkes Night on November 5th for their British employees, and they celebrated Liberation Day on April 25th for their Italian employees.

Usually, most employees liked these celebrations because it was a good opportunity to get together, order some food from the country in question, and spend some time together whilst learning about their colleague's country history and culture. These simple celebrations also reinforced that not everyone came from the same country and the same culture, and it made everyone more aware of cultural differences.

It is also important that team leaders, managers, and leaders remind their employees to show respect for other cultures and languages.

One of the companies I worked with had a team in China and their English was not as good as native speakers. Initially, that led to some jokes, but one leader stepped in and explained that in the company, we celebrate different cultures and languages, and we are proud of having people from different countries. By setting the tone, the team started showing more respect towards each other. When managers draw a line and do not tolerate jokes about language skills, they become role models for the rest of the team and create a more united environment.

Taking into account language fluency and national communication norms is vital when trying to develop a successful team in a hybrid work environment. It helps employees better understand their own culture and adjust their communication style, it helps build rapport between colleagues from different cultures, and it helps reduce stereotypes and improve relationships. By considering language training for your team, using simple language, avoiding jargon and not repeating yourself, and by discussing cultural differences and showing respect, you can

Figure 7.4   Avoid using jargon and idioms and replace them with simple language.

help your hybrid team become more aware of language differences and national communication norms, which will help unify your international team in a hybrid work environment.

Address Conflict Immediately

A few years ago, a large US software vendor contacted me to help them address some issues they were having with their 'international team'. The company was headquartered in the

San Francisco area and had been growing massively over the past few years, which led them to opening offices in Europe and in Asia. However, as the team grew so fast, they started noticing some friction between their employees in headquarters and their employees based outside of their headquarters, in what they called 'Team International'. In particular, the team based in San Francisco complained that their colleagues in China were not participating in meetings, didn't make decisions, and were stopping them from delivering on their projects. The managers in China reported that their US colleagues kept changing their mind, were not clear on their expectations, and didn't provide enough clarity and guidelines on the projects where they needed support. In addition, the Chinese team complained that their US colleagues were often talking over each other in meetings and interrupting one another, making it difficult for them to understand who was driving the conversation and what was being said. As a result, that team often delivered projects late, the managers on both sides were frustrated, and the tone in communication was getting accusatory and very negative.

Conflicts caused by cultural differences are not new and have been disrupting businesses for centuries. On 7 May 1998, German automotive giant Daimler-Benz AG signed a historic merger agreement with American automotive leader Chrysler Corporation. This famous deal was often referred to as the 'merger of equals' at the time. Sadly, the merger became known as a 'fiasco', and the merger, which was initially valued at $35bn, ended up being valued at just $7.4bn nine years later. Many business analysts pointed out that 'discordant company cultures' were the cause of the conflicts inside the organization. In particular, there were sharp differences in the level of formality, approach on topics such as salary and expenses, and in communication styles between the German and American teams. Reports say that the German culture became the dominant one, and Chrysler employees left the organization. A German DaimlerChrysler board member talked about differing behavioural habits and attitudes that annoyed both teams.[15] The board member also revealed that the American colleagues showed 'a complete lack of understanding of German values, methods and working culture'. According to him, American teams found that the Germans 'shook hands too much, were often too intense and followed rigid manuals and rule books'. He also shared that Americans were frustrated with the German's habits of sharing 'constructive criticism'. Germans would take long holidays, which irritated their American colleagues, especially in times of difficulty.

Cultural conflicts can also arise between teams from the same country but from different cultural backgrounds. In 2005, American Telecommunications company Sprint Corporation based in Kansas acquired its competitor Nextel, another American Telecommunications company based in Northern Virginia, in a historic deal reaching $35bn. However, just three years later, the merger had lost 80% of its value! Most business analysts blame the culture clash between the two companies for the failure of the union. Nextel company culture was known as entrepreneurial, while Sprint was known as a formal and bureaucratic organization. An article written by Gigaom said that 'Some Nextel employees say they feel the aggressive, entrepreneurial style that spurred its early growth has been stamped out by Sprint's more bureaucratic approach.' In 2007, *The Washington Post* wrote about the Sprint/Nextel merger fiasco in these words: 'The cultural clash, meanwhile, continues to be an issue at the company'. The newspaper also wrote about the more traditional and 'buttoned-down' way of running the company at Sprint, which clashed with the entrepreneurial culture at Nextel.[16]

There are many examples of conflicts in teams that are due to a clash of culture, as described above. So what exactly are workplace conflicts caused by cultural differences in teams, and what are the risks of not addressing them? Cultural conflicts in teams can take place when people from very different cultural backgrounds work together, especially if they hold very different views on hierarchy and values, and especially when they have not received any training or development programmes on cross-cultural awareness, unconscious bias, and diversity and inclusion. Cross-cultural conflicts can arise when employees with widely different ethnic or cultural backgrounds work closely together as part of the same team because they may operate with very different communication styles, have different work ethics, and value very different things. When the team is subject to a crisis in the organization, a tight deadline, or some stress, those conflicts caused by different cultures can escalate. It goes without saying that cultural conflicts at work are very undesirable; cross cultural conflict is very divisive and hinders collaboration and productivity. Harvard Business School Assistant Professor Roy Y. J. Chua studied how cultural disharmony undermines workplace creativity. Chua wrote a case study about a Chinese luxury apparel company that had employees from China, Hong Kong, Germany, and France working together. Chua noticed some tensions and miscommunication based on cultural differences.[17] Chua coined the term 'ambient cultural disharmony' to describe the work climate caused by cultural tensions. Chua explains: 'A lot of times when we study cultural conflict, it's about people directly involved in conflict,' says Chua. 'The key word here is "ambient", looking at the effect that cultural conflicts can have on an observer. That flows more through the perceptions we have about other cultures.' In a series of experiments that Chua ran, he found that participants who have more people in their social networks from different cultures who disliked each other performed worse on tests about connecting disparate ideas across cultures. He found that ambient cultural disharmony decreased creativity. Chua also found in his previous research that awareness of our own cultural biases can help improve creativity in multicultural situations.

As suggested by Chua, cultural conflicts should be addressed by managers as soon as possible to avoid escalations. There are many risks to the business caused by unaddressed cultural conflicts. Unaddressed cultural conflicts significantly decrease productivity. This can be explained because cultural conflicts can cause employees to leave organizations, causing higher employee turnover rates for organizations that do not address cultural conflicts. Companies with a healthy corporate culture report, on average, a turnover rate of just 13.9% compared to 48.4% at companies with a poor culture, according to a study by Columbia University.[18] Unaddressed cultural conflicts also create divided teams and unhealthy confrontations at work. When cultural conflicts are unresolved, like in the case of the Daimler/Chrysler merger, the different parties remain opponents. The animosity between parties impacts meetings, projects, and the overall productivity of the business unit. Divided teams with unresolved cultural conflicts are unable to collaborate effectively. What's worse is that unresolved cultural conflicts in teams can cause escalations. This is because feelings of animosity that are not addressed become stronger and are more likely to escalate when the team experiences more stress, deadlines, and pressure than usual. Finally, unresolved cultural conflicts lead to a bad reputation of the team and its manager in the organization. When teams are unable to resolve cultural conflicts at work, the rest of the organization will associate that team with a lack of management and with a bad reputation.

Figure 7.5   Address conflict immediately.

Therefore, successful teams proactively deal with cultural conflicts when they arise. In a hybrid work environment, there are a few strategies that you can use to address cultural conflicts immediately as soon as they arise:

- **Document the conflict and gather the facts**
  One of the first steps to addressing conflicts in a hybrid team is to methodically document the conflict and gather the facts. You might consider contacting each team member involved in the conflict and have a conversation individually to gather information about the issue. The goal here is simply to gather information so that you have as much objective data as possible about the issue. Explain to your team members what you have observed about the situation and ask open questions. As you document the conflict, be sure to be consistent with all the parties involved. Share the same message with everyone, explain that your intent is simply to gather the facts, and use the same statement each time you meet with parties to gather information. Ensure that you always ask open questions in order to let all parties come to you with as much information as possible. For example, you can ask employees what has been happening for them, or what they think the next steps of the resolution should be, or who they think should be involved in the resolution. The key when documenting the conflict is to know your intention, which is to find the facts and to act as an objective facilitator or conflict mediator.

- **Acknowledge and discuss conflict openly**
  In a remote or hybrid work setting, many conflicts happen because long-standing issues have

been unresolved due to managers not noticing them and/or not addressing them. The most successful hybrid teams have managers who acknowledge conflicts and discuss them openly with their teams to resolve them proactively. When team leaders take the first step to resolve the conflict, they take a proactive approach towards conflict resolution, which, in itself, is half the battle already won. Use regular team meetings to discuss any issue that needs to be addressed. Once you have acknowledged and discussed existing tensions in the team, make sure you also celebrate team success to set the tone and encourage teamwork and collaboration. You might also discuss team conflicts online on a Slack channel if many of your team members work remotely and in a different time zone, so that you can discuss the issue quicker than waiting to arrange a meeting. Ask everyone for their input to solve the issue and reinforce that the intent is to solve the problem, not to point fingers.

> Using online channels can help solve conflicts faster by getting more instant feedback and removing inhibitions, because some people are more likely to share their thoughts online than in a meeting.

- **Set ground rules and act as a role model**

    An important strategy to address conflict at work is to set clear ground rules and to embrace these rules by acting as a role model. These rules can include some of the following statements:

    ◆ Treat all your co-workers with respect and fairness, including those from different backgrounds, cultures, and with different languages.

- Listen to your colleagues' views including if they are different from yours; when your view differs from your colleagues, say it and explain why.

- When in doubt, ensure that you are aligned with your colleagues before moving forward on a project; when you do or say something wrong, apologize.

- Participate in open and constructive dialogue; pick your battles.

These are just a few examples of ground rules that you should share with your team members about your approach to conflict and conflict prevention. Of course, there are more ground rules that you can share with your team, and you should feel free to share as many (or as little) as you wish, but the main point is to set some ground rules and share them to prevent conflicts in your team. Modelling these rules will reinforce them and send the message that you walk the walk yourself. If you say to your team: 'When you do or say something wrong, apologize', but you never apologize yourself when you make a mistake, chances are that your team won't apologize either when they do something wrong. On the other hand, if you tell your team: 'When your view differs from your colleagues, say it and explain why', and you always share openly your different views during team meetings and explain your reasoning, your team is more likely to emulate your behaviour and to challenge their colleagues' opinions in meetings, explaining why they disagree. Great role models do good things outside of the job as well, meaning that they continue to act as positive role models outside of their nine-to-five shifts.

The best role models I have come across in my consulting career are those who are not afraid to acknowledge their weaknesses and limitations; they say sorry when they did something wrong, and they ask for feedback often to improve their skills.

• **Track productivity and pay attention to small details**

One of the most effective strategies to address conflict is to track the productivity of your team and to pay attention to small details. This is because workplace conflicts cause stress and disruption, damage relationships, affect employee morale, and can even impact customer service. As a result, when conflict arises, your team productivity plummets. By monitoring your team's productivity closely and paying attention to your team's key performance indicators, you will be able to react quickly and check if any conflict has arisen and impacted your team's collaboration. In a hybrid work environment, this includes paying attention to who remains quiet in meetings the entire time, noticing if someone who used to come to the office often suddenly avoids the office and works from home all the time, paying attention to any change in the dynamic of your team meetings, and noticing the tone of the emails in your team. By paying attention to your team interactions, and by monitoring your team productivity closely, you will be able to prevent conflicts before they arise or address them as soon as they arise, avoiding escalations.

In a highly international environment, where people from different cultures work together, conflicts can arise and they can linger more in a virtual setting. If unaddressed, workplace conflicts due to a culture clash can damage the business, as in the case of the Daimler/Chrysler merger, where the American teams and the German teams simply could not continue to work together and caused major disruption in the organization. By taking proactive steps to address conflict immediately in a hybrid work environment, managers can help unify their cross-cultural hybrid teams and attract, develop, and retain a successful team. Simple strategies including documenting the conflict and gathering the facts, acknowledging and discussing conflicts openly, setting ground rules and acting as a role model, and tracking productivity and paying attention to small details can significantly help address conflict effectively in a virtual work environment.

Encourage Team-Building Activities and Build Rapport

At the start of the Covid-19 pandemic, when most employees had to shift to remote-work virtually overnight, Seattle-based sales and marketing technology company Highspot experienced a boom in after-hours team-building activities, such as virtual happy hours. Jennifer Palecki, Vice President of People for Highspot, recalls: 'before the pandemic, all Highspot employees came together for an hour-long lunch every Friday'.[19] During the pandemic, Highspot employees started doing the same virtually, because the company 'keeps that time sacred'. What's even more remarkable is that out of the 500 employees working at the company, 350 to 400 of them attend it each time! Palecki shares another way that the company encourages team-building activities to build connections in a virtual world: each week, company executives dedicate two hours to be available virtually to any employee who wants to have a one-to-one chat. As Palecki comments: 'it emulates hallway conversations.'

Highspot is not the only company that embraced team-building activities during the Covid-19 pandemic. Online retail company Zappos had always built its company culture on intentional team-building activities, so when the pandemic happened, the company had to find ways to build rapport in a hybrid work environment. Zappos built a 'fun-gineering' team to build fun and rapport virtually. The online retailer started hosting 90-minute virtual events that any employee could sign up for. The fun-gineering team even added a physical dimension by sending a gift box to each participant. These virtual events have proved very popular and get quickly booked by employees. One particularly fun virtual team-building event hosted by Zappos is called the 'Worst Cooks' event. The company ships ingredients to employees who want to take part and asks participants to cook a meal and share videos, which are then shared company-wide.

Many companies have embraced team-building activities for virtual teams during the Covid-19 pandemic. From technology companies to online retailers, many businesses have invested in activities that build rapport and connection in a virtual world. Virtual team-building activities are activities that build connections, rapport, and trust between employees, that are conducted in a virtual environment. They can include group games, contests, or exercises and can take place on virtual platforms such as Zoom, Microsoft Teams, Google Meet, or other. Virtual team building, also known as online team building, brings unity to virtual teams by building psychological safety among team members who might not be able to build rapport otherwise.

There are many significant benefits to virtual team-building activities in the organization. During the Covid-19 pandemic, many organizations turned to virtual team building as a way to connect their employees who felt more isolated and more disconnected from their peers due to remote and hybrid work. The benefits of virtual team-building activities have been remarkable, as per the survey by Team Building Hub shared in 2022: Team Building Hub conducted a research study with professionals dedicated to virtual team building and found that 63% of leaders felt team communication improved after participating in team-building activities, and 61% of leaders felt team morale improved.[20] The study also revealed that 55% of leaders feel team culture would improve if their company invested more in team building, and most importantly, 73% of employees wish their company would invest more in team building. The Team Building Hub survey found that at companies investing less than $25 per month per person in team building, 58% of employees feel that morale is 'ok', 'bad', or 'very bad'.

At companies investing more than $25 per month per person in team building, only 25% of employees feel that morale is 'ok', 'bad', or 'very bad'. The research is clear: investing in team building drastically improves employee morale, team culture, and communication, especially in virtual teams. Team-building activities help connect remote and hybrid teams; this is because it helps build stronger relationships. When people work together from different locations, different countries, and different cultures, taking the time to organize team-building activities will help them build stronger relationships outside of work which, in turn, will have a big impact on how people interact moving forward. Team-building activities also help boost motivation and employee engagement. This is because when a group of people complete a challenge together, they are able to bond and to become more engaged with one another; it also adds an element of fun that often gets lost in the day-to-day work, so it brings a very welcome element of enjoyment and entertainment to the team dynamics. Team-building activities also boost team collaboration and productivity, because employees trust each other more, better understand each other, and are more effective in their communication afterwards. Because of a greater sense of trust and psychological safety brought in by team-building activities, teams become more creative and innovative. When the group comes together around quizzes, games, and contests, the people build a greater sense of safety and feel more secure to speak their mind freely without fear of being criticized or judged. This leads to more ideas being shared, more creativity in the team and even more innovation.

In an interview for *Forbes* magazine, Jenny Gottstein, director of games at The Go Game, a new interactive and creative approach to team building, reveals why leading companies such as Uber, Facebook, Salesforce, and Johnson & Johnson invest heavily in team building activities.[21] Gottstein explains: 'The best way to engage employees is to build a culture of trust. Nothing is more isolating and damaging than a fear of taking risks or voicing one's opinion.' The team-building expert explains that effective team-building activities foster a culture of trust. Gottstein also explains how team building turns workers into company advocates, which helps attract and retain top talent.

In a hybrid work environment, it can be more challenging to implement team-building activities that will unify international hybrid teams; the most effective types of team-building activities happen face-to-face, which might not always be possible in a virtual work environment when colleagues are geographically dispersed over different countries or even continents. However, it is possible to leverage team-building activities in a hybrid work environment; below are some of the most effective ways to implement team building in hybrid teams that I have observed:

- **Hold regular non-work-related chats**

    In a hybrid team, where some employees have never met face-to-face with their co-workers, it can be particularly challenging to build rapport in a natural way. A 2020 survey by Aetna International found that 40% of employers say they're concerned that a lack of social interaction among colleagues will have a long-term negative impact on some employees' mental health.[22] Social interaction between colleagues, especially in a non-work-related context, significantly improves employees' well-being, engagement, and sense of belonging. The now famous Harvard Study of Adult Development studied the lives of 724 men for 79 years, to uncover the secret to success, happiness, and a good life. The study found that relationships have a significant impact on people's health, happiness, and quality of life. It also found that the quality of relationships matters more than quantity.[23] When managers facilitate group conversations that are non-work-related, they help their team members to build rapport, to strengthen their relationships, and to become more socially connected and happier. In a virtual world, this can be done by hosting weekly chats to talk about the weekend ahead for example. You can host a Friday 'weekend plans' Zoom call to talk about your team members' plans for the weekend. If possible, you can make it more inviting by sending each of your team members a voucher to order their lunch at their desk, so that people can share a virtual lunch together and talk about their hobbies, their families, or their interests outside of work. By hosting weekly chats over Zoom that are non-work-related, you will help your team members build rapport and unify your team through socializing. You can also host bi-weekly chats if weekly feels too much for your team. Ask your team members what day of the week and what time works best for them; think about ways to encourage participations – you can make it a company-wide tradition so that all teams use the same time to socialize, etc.

- **Host annual trips to exciting locations**

  If your team is fully remote, or even if your team is hybrid, chances are that they are not very close to each other and have not had a chance to build strong relationships by sharing lunch, coffees, and office banter. By facilitating a face-to-face gathering for your entire team in an exotic location, you will be able to foster very strong relationships in your team that would not otherwise be possible. Annie McKee, author of

How to Be Happy at Work, explained that 'one of the ways we can make ourselves happy and feel more fulfilled in our workplaces is to build friendships with the people that work with us, work for us and even with our boss'.[24] It sounds obvious and simple; however, in order to build friendships at work in a virtual world, the most effective strategy is to host a team event in an exciting location. Start with an annual trip and build on this. During that team retreat, schedule some team-bonding activities and some free time for people to plan their own schedules as well.

UK Investment company Connection Capital has embraced annual team retreats and it's proven so beneficial for the team that the company has been doing it every year. In a press release, Connection Capital explained: 'We think it's important to remove them from the settings of their day-to-day business and give them the opportunity to hear from other entrepreneurs and inspirational speakers. We find this distance helps create perspective with which to look back and think about the future plans for their business.'[25] The UK investment firm usually hosts their annual retreat over a two-day period, inviting keynote speakers to share inspiring stories, hosting some workshop sessions and dinners, and some fun activities such as rounds of golf, wine tasting sessions, and a coffee tasting class. They also include some executive coaching sessions as well as some business-related activities. Essentially, hosting annual trips in exotic locations help the team become more unified, especially if they work in a virtual work setting most of the time.

- **Incorporate cultural awareness in your team-building plan**

  If your team works primarily virtually, with very few opportunities to meet face-to-face, it is very likely that the level of camaraderie and rapport between team members is not very high, and if you have team members from different cultural backgrounds, your team is probably experiencing some miscommunication and frictions due to a lack of cultural awareness of each other's backgrounds. By incorporating a cultural awareness element into your team-building strategy, you will increase the level of cultural awareness, which will help your international team come together as 'one team'. For example, you can celebrate traditional holidays, national days, and food from the countries where some of your team members are from. You can do some team-building activities focused on selling or marketing to a new country or a new continent; you can host a cooking class focusing on a cuisine from the area where some of your team members live; you can ask each team member to share a presentation on the norms, cultural standards, and habits of the country they are from, and how they differ from the country your company is headquartered in, for example. The main goal is to bring an element of cultural awareness into your team-building activities, so that your team becomes more aware of some of the subtle cultural differences that exist and therefore are more mindful of these in their communication moving forward.

Encouraging team-building activities and building rapport in a team in a hybrid work environment might seem challenging because of the physical distance between employees, the lack of opportunities for casual conversations, and the increased feeling of isolation and disconnection that's more prevalent in a virtual work environment. However, research shows that 73% of employees wish their company would invest more in team building, and this appetite for team-building activities is even more prominent in virtual teams, who have even fewer opportunities to build rapport through casual conversations, lunches, and coffee breaks.

Investing in team-building activities is really fundamental to truly unify a cross-cultural hybrid team, and it should be done with a dimension of cultural awareness. When team leaders facilitate regular non-work-related chats, host annual trips to exciting locations, and incorporate cultural awareness in their team-building plans, they are able to unify their international teams in a way that will foster better collaboration, trust, respect, and productivity.

Employees are also more likely to stay in organizations and teams when they feel a stronger sense of belonging and a team spirit, which is vital in a hybrid work setting. As Patrick Lencioni famously said: 'Teamwork begins by building trust. And the only way to do that is to overcome our need for invulnerability.'

Conclusion

Many studies have been conducted on the effect of cross-cultural differences on team performance, productivity, and collaboration. These studies demonstrate the many benefits of working with international colleagues; from improved performance due to innovation and creativity, to a more open-minded approach to challenges and opportunities, to flexibility and agility. An international, diverse team simply performs better. However, managing a highly international team, which is often the case for organizations that operate in a hybrid work model, can also present some challenges. In particular, when these highly international teams operate in a virtual work environment (through hybrid work or through remote work), it can be difficult for managers and team leaders to unify their team around a shared language, shared communication, and with a good rapport. The Covid-19 pandemic accelerated the need to unify multicultural teams in a way that is scalable. The forced remote-work revolution that took place during the Covid-19 pandemic pushed leaders to find new ways to unify their international teams in a virtual work environment.

Leaders of international hybrid teams are starting to promote psychological safety and inclusion. Companies like Google have studied the link between psychological safety in teams and performance and are embracing strategies to build psychological safety in their teams. Leaders are starting to set the tone and lead the way to show what psychological safety looks like in hybrid work. Leaders like Jeff Bezos at Amazon are often used as examples of successful teams with psychological safety, with his famous 'Tell me even more candidly' sign on his office door. Team leaders today also help their people connect to build a layer of trust that allows more honest conversations and healthy conflicts; the best leaders constantly watch out for harmful comments that may destroy the level of psychological safety and trust in their team;

managers who follow these guidelines are able to promote high levels of psychological safety and inclusion in their hybrid teams, which in turn unifies their team.

In addition to promoting trust, the best leaders also build strategic cross-cultural awareness programmes to unify their hybrid teams. Leading technology firms such as IBM have been embracing training programmes about cultural norms of nations, including their famous 'country navigator' programme, for years; more companies have been following them since the shift to remote and hybrid work, to allow their employees to better understand cultural differences and communication styles, especially in hybrid work. Airplane manufacturing leader Boeing also implemented initiatives to raise awareness about cultural diversity, with their 'GlobeSmart' programme, which is an online resource for employees to learn about cultural norms of different countries. The most successful companies plan for success by integrating their cultural awareness programmes into their existing communication channels. Some team leaders also use storytelling to increase cultural awareness in their hybrid teams, and some practise culturally aware communication by removing jargon and colloquialisms from their everyday language.

More companies are also reconsidering language fluency in their hybrid team to unify their employees in a hybrid work environment. An increasing number of organizations are investing in language training to boost confidence in non-native English speakers and improve communication between members of different cultures. Many team leaders are becoming 'chief reminder officers', repeating themselves to ensure that their message is well understood by every member of their teams. More international companies are also discussing cultural diversity and emphasize showing respect to everyone; as a result, hybrid teams become more aware of language differences and national communication norms, which help unify them in a highly distributed work environment.

As teams become more hybrid and hire employees from different countries and different continents, conflicts can arise due to cultural differences and norms, so companies are also addressing conflicts to build unified teams in a hybrid work environment. Some of the best leaders use simple steps to proactively address tensions in their hybrid teams, including documenting the conflict and gathering the facts, acknowledging and discussing the conflict openly, setting ground rules and acting as a role model, and tracking productivity and paying attention to small details.

Finally, more organizations are discovering the power of team-building activities for hybrid teams and are investing in it to unify their people in a virtual work environment. Successful companies like Highspot and Zappos are investing people and resources in team building, in particular since the shift to remote work. These companies are holding regular non-work-related chats for their teams with great success and attendance from their employees. Other companies are hosting annual trips to exciting locations, such as investment company Connection Capital; some organizations are incorporating cultural awareness in their team-building plans and celebrate important national holidays and cultural events as a team. As a result, employees working in hybrid teams are more likely to stay in organizations and teams when they feel a stronger sense of belonging and team spirit.

As the workplace is experiencing the third revolution since the Covid-19 pandemic, and since the adoption of hybrid work, the need for unity amongst remote employees from different cultures has never been greater. An increasing number of employees are feeling isolated and disconnected from the group, with a lack of belonging and sometimes a feeling that their native communication style and cultural norms are not accepted or celebrated by their peers, a withdrawal from conversations and from sharing ideas, some misunderstandings, tensions and conflicts, and a sense of exclusion. An increasing number of leading organizations including Google, IBM, Boeing, Highspot, and Zappos are investing in strategies to increase unity in their hybrid teams; they focus more on promoting psychological safety, improving cross-cultural awareness, considering language fluency, addressing conflicts when they arise, and encouraging team building. As a result, these companies are maintaining their positions as market leaders in their fields, and their employees' Net Promoter Scores are amongst the best in the market. As the greatest basketball player in the history of the sport, Michael Jordan, said: 'Talent wins games, but teamwork and intelligence win championships.' This could not be more true in a hybrid team, where the need for teamwork and unity is greater than ever before.

Endnotes

1. https://www.zoho.com/blog/general/what-i-learned-from-working-remotely-with-cross-cultural-teams.html

2. https://www.researchgate.net/publication/328942701_Psychological_Safety_and_Collective_Intelligence_in_Multicultural_Globally_Dispersed_Teams

3. https://www.graduate.technion.ac.il/Theses/Abstracts. asp?Id=28236

4. https://rework.withgoogle.com/blog/five-keys-to-a-successful-google-team/

5. https://psychologischeveiligheid.net/cgblog/24/49/How-a-tough-company-like-Amazon-fosters-psychological-safety

6. http://oictoday.biz/business-details.php?id=72/create-a-crosscultural-training-programme-that-works

7. https://www.shrm.org/hr-today/news/hr-magazine/pages/010215-cross-cultural-training.aspx

8. Ibid.

9. https://elearningindustry.com/reasons-you-should-be-telling-stories-in-your-training

10. https://hbr.org/2015/10/when-culture-doesnt-translate

11. https://resources.rosettastone.com/assets/lp/9999999999/resources/5-reasons-leaders-invest-in-language-training.pdf

12. https://www.td.org/insights/5-ways-language-training-improves-employee-performance

13. https://resources.rosettastone.com/assets/lp/9999999999/resources/5-reasons-leaders-invest-in-language-training.pdf

14. https://www.td.org/insights/5-ways-language-training-improves-employee-performance

15. https://www.crossculture.com/cross-cultural-issues-at-the-daimlerchrysler-merge-case-study/

16. https://www.washingtonpost.com/archive/
business/2007/02/23/sprint-nextels-spotty-
connection-span-classbankheadfrom-corporate-
culture-to-marketing-merged-company-has-yet-to-
meshspan/95baeac6-84ef-42cb-84bd-bda9f0c017bb/

17. https://hbswk.hbs.edu/item/cultural-
disharmony-undermines-workplace-creativity

18. https://pollackpeacebuilding.com/workplace-
conflict-statistics/

19. https://www.shrm.org/hr-today/news/all-things-work/
pages/building-stronger-teams-virtually.aspx

20. https://teambuildinghub.com/blog/team-
building-statistics/

21. https://www.forbes.com/sites/kathycaprino
/2016/01/14/how-companies-like-uber-facebook-
and-salesforce-engage-in-team-building-its-not-what-
you-think/?sh=7e3a611b3cc1

22. https://www.quantumworkplace.com/future-of-work/
remote-work-statistics

23. https://www.forbes.com/sites/alankohll/2018/01/31/5-ways-
social-connections-can-enhance-your-employee-
wellness-program/?sh=3cbe9fed527c

24. McKee, A. (2018). How to Be Happy at Work.
Boston, MA: Havard Business Review Press.

25. https://www.connectioncapital.co.uk/news/
connection-capital-host-annual-management-team-
retreat-in-gleneagles/

Appendix

Leveraging Meetings in Hybrid Work

Figure A.1   Leveraging meetings in hybrid work.

When Vanessa Moss, astronomer at Australia's national science agency, recalls some of the hybrid work meetings she had to join, she talks about some of the challenges she faced. Vanessa recalls having a difficult time following along due to 'choppy audio feeds or people in the office sitting too far from microphones'.[1] She also remembers that in some hybrid meetings, the remote meeting attendees, including herself, were often forgotten by the in-person attendees, who dominated the conversation. Vanessa (and the other remote meeting attendees) often heard laughter and chatter from the in-person meeting participants, whom she could not see very well either. Like many, she felt isolated and disempowered. 'Your voice isn't heard so you translate it into your feelings or thoughts don't matter', said Vanessa.

Vanessa Moss is not the only victim of badly run hybrid meetings: the majority of employees who have joined hybrid meetings have experienced similar issues. Collaboration software Asana gathered its executives during the Covid-19 pandemic for a discussion about the office reopening. Half of the meeting participants were at the office in San Francisco, and the other half joined by video conference. The remote attendees, including the CEO, started to lose their patience as people in the office talked over one another and made side comments. Even the company's Head of People Anne Binder commented that they (the remote meeting attendees) were joking that if they didn't like what somebody said on the screen, they could just mute them. Binder commented: 'We all had such a terrible experience that we made a decision at the end of that meeting that all executive meetings going forward will be in-person.' She continued, 'Or they will be fully remote. We're not doing the in-between.'[2]

Holding hybrid meetings can present many challenges, many of which are relatively new for people. First, hybrid meetings make it very challenging to maintain high levels of engagement for all participants. Remote meeting participants may struggle more to remain engaged throughout; they may have more distractions (package delivery, doorbell ringing, relatives or roommates' interruptions, pets, etc.) and as a result they are more likely to be multitasking. If remote meeting participants are not invited to contribute, they are more likely to be disengaged in the meeting.

Hybrid meetings can also be a barrier to collaboration and teamwork; when meeting participants are in different physical locations, creating a united team that works as a unit can be more challenging than usual. From internet lag to technical issues related to audio or video to poor connectivity, hybrid meetings can be a challenge and contribute to miscommunication or bottlenecks. The security element of hybrid meetings is also a challenge that can prevent teams from being as collaborative and as productive as before. The risks of sensitive data leaking, ransomware, cybersecurity issues, and malware are much higher in hybrid meetings than in traditional face-to-face meetings. This is especially true for hybrid meetings that discuss sensitive information such as board meetings, business review meetings, quarterly business reviews, performance reviews, and HR meetings. Sensitive data, including financial information, data about employees, salaries, profit and loss, and financial performance, are more likely to be leaked, stolen, or used for ransomware attacks in hybrid work meetings. As a result, some hybrid meeting participants might be reluctant to share information and to contribute for fear of putting confidential information at risk; this can lead to productivity issues, communication issues and, of course, cybersecurity issues. Hybrid meetings can also contribute to feelings of exclusion for those who are full-time remote employees. Remote meeting participants can feel left out, isolated, and even excluded from the main conversation, because they are often 'out of sight, out of mind' and simply forgotten by the meeting attendees who are in the office. As a result, they may not be asked for their input during meetings, or they may be given just a few minutes at the end of the meeting to share their thoughts, when their co-workers in the office had plenty of time to contribute.

Hybrid meetings are what brings hybrid teams together. In a hybrid work environment, they are the vehicle for team collaboration, communication, team building, and creativity. Hybrid meetings involve a combination of in-person and remote meeting participants. Remote participants join the conversation via a video conferencing platform such as Zoom or Microsoft Teams, whereas in-person participants are together in a meeting room in the office. Hybrid meetings are different from remote or virtual meetings, where all participants join remotely (from home or from another location). Hybrid meetings are a unique mix of office components and virtual components. The goal is to facilitate smooth discussion and collaboration and make those things as easy as in a face-to-face meeting. The trend for hybrid meetings is on the rise, especially since the Covid-19 pandemic started in March 2020. According to an article titled 'Addressing the Biggest Challenges of Hosting Hybrid Events' published by *Harvard Business Review*, 'In 2021, 64% of businesses say they're increasing their virtual events, and 58% say they're planning for a mix of virtual and in-person events.'[3] In an article published by *Forbes* and titled 'Four Reasons Your Company Should Pivot To Hybrid Events', leading speakers bureau All American Entertainment surveyed its clients about their 2021 event plans, and it revealed that 'about two-thirds of those surveyed said they are actively moving ahead with in-person, virtual, and hybrid event planning for 2021'.[4] In a survey ran by Cisco titled 'The Rise of the Hybrid Workplace: A Global Survey of Executives, Employee Experience Experts, and Knowledge Workers' published in October 2020, it was found that 98% of those surveyed expect all meetings to include remote participants.

With the majority of knowledge workers choosing to continue working remotely as much as possible, hybrid meetings are here to stay. There are some very good reasons and benefits for it as well! First, hybrid meetings can significantly boost efficiency. They can allow employees to reduce travel time, and they can join more meetings if they don't have to travel between each one. It also allows more employees to join meetings because a more diverse group of people can now join, even if they are not physically located in the same office. hybrid meetings are also more inclusive than traditional office meetings because they allow employees to join remotely, who would not otherwise be able to work. For example, parents caring for young children can do the school run in the morning and in the afternoon can work remotely, having the flexibility to work and care for their children at the same time. Disabled individuals no longer have to face the commute to work as they can now join meetings remotely. Individuals living in remote neighbourhoods due to lower incomes can now join meetings remotely without having to face an expensive commute every day. Hybrid meetings simply give more employees access to work and are therefore more equitable and more inclusive than traditional in-person meetings; they are also more convenient because they can be recorded, rewatched, and shared with more people afterwards. Hybrid meetings are also much more cost-effective than off-site meetings at expensive venues; if your organization embraces hybrid meetings and hybrid work, it will probably downsize its office space and save important office costs for your organization. However, as mentioned previously, there is a real risk if hybrid meetings are not run inclusively; if remote participants are not proactively invited to the conversation, remain quiet the entire meeting, or only have a few minutes to share their input compared to their in-office colleagues, you may unconsciously create a two-tiered workforce: one where in-office employees are more included and recognized, and remote employees are more excluded and underappreciated. So you must follow a few strategies to ensure that your hybrid meetings are inclusive, equitable, and optimized for your hybrid team:

- **Appoint hybrid meeting facilitators**
  Hybrid meetings always present a risk for remote meeting participants that they will not be heard, valued, or included as much as their office colleagues. A study of 1000 employees recently conducted by Business Electricity Prices found that '53% of remote employees are worried about being left out of in-person team meetings and other activities that take place in the office'.[5] Another study titled '2019 State of the Digital Workspace' by software firm Igloo found that 70% of remote workers feel left out of the workplace.[6]

Remote employees are indeed feeling more excluded and left out from hybrid meetings than their office counterparts, and for good reason: they are much more likely to be forgotten, excluded, and not paid attention to during hybrid meetings. This is why appointing a meeting facilitator for all your hybrid meetings is key to creating an inclusive and equitable meeting experience for all meeting participants, not just in-office workers.

Meeting facilitators lead the meeting and foster rapport between participants; they also provide direction and reframe the conversation to ensure that it stays on track. Their mission is also to monitor the conversation and ensure equitable participation from all meeting participants, including remote workers.

Meeting facilitators also pay attention to group dynamics to ensure that diverse perspectives are being heard, and not just perspectives from the loudest and the most extrovert or the most senior participants. Meeting, facilitators also take notes, share agendas before the meeting, and share summaries and actions after the meeting to communicate well with all meeting participants before, during, and after the meeting.

- **Pay attention to details**

  As Vanessa Moss explained when she joined hybrid meetings remotely, working at Australia's national science agency, she often heard laughter and chatter from the in-person meeting participants whilst not being able to participate at all. These side conversations can really impact how remote participants feel in hybrid meetings, making them feel more excluded and isolated. When hosting hybrid meetings, pay attention to details such as side conversations and side jokes from office participants that exclude remote meeting participants. Don't be afraid to speak up and say, 'I'm hearing a lot of side conversations which are excluding our remote participants, can we make sure we speak to the entire group?' Likewise, if you notice that some remote participants unmute themselves, or try to make a point and get into the conversation but they struggle, call it out. You may say: 'I noticed that Sarah unmuted herself, and Jane was trying to say something; Sarah, Jane, what would you like to say?'

> By paying attention to small details such as side conversations, meeting participants unmuting themselves, or remote employees struggling to get into the conversation, you will host a more inclusive hybrid meeting that will make all your participants feel included and part of the conversation.

- **Use the round-robin method**
  If you are new to managing hybrid meetings and you have not had a chance to appoint a meeting facilitator just yet, a simple way to ensure that you host an inclusive and equitable meeting is to use the round-robin method. This method, also called round-robin brainstorming, essentially allows everyone to contribute in an equal manner. It allows all meeting participants to share ideas without being influenced by one person. Ask each team member to think about a contribution or

an idea, comment, or feedback they want to share related to the topic of the meeting; ask each meeting participant to share their idea in turn and when they are done, ask the next person to do the same. Once each meeting participant has had a chance to share their idea, continue with this circular contribution swap as long as necessary until the time is up. This simple method allows all remote meeting participants to contribute and speak up as much as in-office meeting participants. It fosters equity and inclusion for remote meeting participants and reminds office participants that they also have colleagues joining remotely.

- **Pair remote workers with office workers**
  Pairing employees is a practice that has existed for a while and has been used across many industries. Many companies pair a new employee, or new starter, with someone who has been working at the company for a while to help the new starter navigate his new workplace more effectively. However, the Covid-19 pandemic has pushed more companies to widen pairing to remote workers. More companies are now pairing remote workers with office workers in an attempt to foster more inclusion in the workplace. These organizations have found that remote team pairing improves collaboration, increases engagement, and boosts morale of both employees. This system is also referred to as the 'buddy system' because it essentially assigns a remote employee a 'buddy' or a friendly person to be their guide in the organization. During hybrid meetings, the office-based buddy stays connected to their remote buddy, invites them to get into the conversation, and notices when the remote buddy is struggling to get in or wants to speak.

The rise of hybrid meetings and events is a trend that continues to grow, in every country, in every industry, and in every organization, no matter how big or small. According to a 2020 Marketing Charts survey, half (50.7%) of executives think that in the future, all live events will possess a virtual dimension.[7] According to a 2020 AMEX study, event organizers reported that 23.6% of their events in 2021 will include a virtual component and will be smaller local events with fewer than 25 attendees who will require no air travel or hotel rooms. Whether your company is planning hybrid events, or whether you simply want to create more inclusive and equitable hybrid meetings, you need to learn how to host hybrid meetings in an inclusive and equitable way. By appointing hybrid meeting facilitators who are trained on keeping equitable practices in a hybrid work environment, by paying attention to small details and dynamics in the group, by using the round-robin method to guarantee equitable speaking time, and by pairing remote workers with office workers, you will host hybrid meetings that are equitable, inclusive, and fair towards your remote workers.

Common Pitfalls of Hybrid Work and How to Overcome Them

When American social news website Reddit decided to adopt remote work and to have a distributed workforce, the company invested in the best video conferencing systems and state-of-the-art remote working tools. The San Francisco–based company spent time learning remote-work best practices from other distributed companies. Although the company found that remote employees did good work and were productive, it decided to end the remote work policy just two years after starting it. CEO Yishan Wong explained, 'As it turns out, our teams (within each office) and remote workers did good work, but the separation has kept us from effectively being able to coordinate as well as we needed to on a full-company level. Big efforts that require quick action, deep understanding, and efficient coordination between people at multiple offices just don't go as well as we (and our users) needed.'[8] In other words, Reddit's CEO claimed that communication suffered because of remote work – speed and problem-solving were negatively affected due to remote working.

Reddit isn't the only company that had a poor experience with hybrid work. American web services provider Yahoo also had an experiment with remote work, which didn't go to plan. Less than a year after joining Yahoo as the CEO, Marissa Mayer suddenly banned remote work in the company. Yahoo's CEO memo announced that remote workers should either relocate close to the office or quit. The memo said that 'to become the absolute best place to work, communication and collaboration will be important, so we need to be working side-by-side. That is why it is critical that we are all present in our offices.' Yahoo's CEO also demanded that even employees working one or two days in the office submit to the new regime of office-based work. The memo explained that 'speed and quality are often sacrificed when we work from home'. However, was the decision to end remote work at Yahoo justified? Some Yahoo employees revealed that there was 'little effort to stay in touch regularly,' suggesting that the company failed to handle internal communication well; another former Yahoo employee shared that working from home actually made them a lot more productive, quoting:

'I didn't have to put up with numbskull self-important programmers constantly yakking to each other LOUDLY from the next set of cubicles about non-work-related stuff, and I wasn't being distracted every 20 minutes by some bored soul coming over to my desk to go for coffee or foosball.'[9]

Hybrid work can present some real challenges, especially for teams and organizations that are not well prepared for it. As the example of Yahoo demonstrates, hybrid work can sometimes struggle with collaboration challenges; Yahoo's CEO cited that 'speed and quality were often sacrificed when we work from home'. Marissa Mayer also said, 'We need to be working side-by-side because communication and collaboration are important. That is why it is critical that we are all present in our offices.' To a certain extent, she is right: when hybrid teams are not managed properly, and not given the right attention and guidelines, their collaboration and communication can suffer. Of course, poor internet connection, working different hours, and living in different countries and continents can also hinder communication and collaboration in hybrid work. Hybrid working can sometimes mean that remote employees have less access to information. If managers have not prepared well by implementing a few best practices to share information, remote workers and hybrid employees may struggle more than their office counterparts to access information easily and on time. Remote and hybrid employees may also be more at risk of not getting promoted or offered career and development opportunities at the same rate as office workers; it might be unintentional and the result of unconscious bias towards remote and hybrid employees, but research has demonstrated that 'out-of-sight' employees are more likely to miss out on career development opportunities as opposed to their office peers. Hybrid work might sometimes lead hybrid and remote employees to feel like they are more excluded and isolated from the team in comparison to their office colleagues; many studies have demonstrated this. A survey of employees conducted by the Royal Society for Public Health found that two-thirds (67%) of workers who shifted from the office to home during the pandemic felt less connected to their colleagues.[10] The same survey also highlighted disparities between different demographics: women were more likely than men to report feeling isolated (58% and 39% respectively). Another study conducted by OnePoll surveyed 2000 work-from-home Americans to explore the social impact of being away from the workplace after more than a year of remote work. It revealed that 7 in 10 employees who work from home are feeling more isolated compared to being in the office. With the absence of in-person events, 63% felt less engaged with their team, as the average employee felt disconnected.[11]

If the common pitfalls of hybrid work environments are not addressed, hybrid teams can suffer greatly from a lack of collaboration, decreased productivity, lower employee morale and engagement, greater employee turnover, bad reputation in the market, and can even fail completely. This is why it is fundamental that hybrid team managers and leaders take some steps to prevent the most frequent issues that can arise in hybrid work. Below are some of the most common pitfalls and issues that can arise in hybrid work and how to overcome them:

- **Collaboration and communication challenges**

In hybrid work, communication tends to be more asynchronous, meaning that it doesn't happen in real-time, but rather, there is a delay between the time the person delivers the message and the time the recipient receives it. A typical example of this is when hybrid teams use instant messaging tools such as Slack-many messengers wait to get a reply to their message. Delayed replies to messages can hinder communication and collaboration, and can also create some silos between in-office workers and remote workers.

By implementing an effective hybrid communication strategy, managers can mitigate the risks of poor communication in hybrid work. First, managers should reassess their current communication framework. By asking a few simple questions – What tools do employees use to communicate each day? What are the guidelines for meetings? What training is provided to employees on communication tools? – managers can get a picture of the areas that require improvement. Leaders should define policies and workflows for the ideal communication in hybrid work, and they should communicate about it often via all channels. Leaders should seek frequent feedback from their teams on areas for improvement related to communication, both qualitative and quantitative. Team leaders should host frequent 'lunch and learn' sessions and invite the entire team to discuss communication and collaboration successes and areas for improvement. Team leaders should also leverage team meetings and one-to-ones to ensure that all employees are included in the relevant projects.

- **Access to information and knowledge**

    In January 2022, a Gartner research paper titled
'Checklist for Ensuring Hybrid Workers Can Always
Find the Information They Need' revealed that 'Among
the biggest barriers to productivity for remote and
hybrid workers is the inability to find the information
they need for their day-to-day work.[12] This problem is
exacerbated by the lack of 'walking-around
knowledge' – that is, knowledge gained by asking
colleagues questions during casual encounters in, for
example, the cafeteria or corridor.' For knowledge
workers, having instant and easy access to important
information is key to doing their job effectively and
efficiently. However, many companies have struggled to
make access to information and knowledge easy and
simple in hybrid work. Companies such as Yahoo and
Reddit have blamed a lack of access to information and
knowledge for failing at remote work.

    Team leaders can follow a few simple steps to
make information accessible to everyone in hybrid
work. Firstly, managers should ensure that they build
an effective onboarding process. Quality and proven
onboarding processes set teams up for success when it
comes to information sharing. Managers should also
reinforce the guidelines of information sharing by
following the guidelines themselves. When managers
actually follow the rules themselves, their team
members are much more likely to follow in their
footsteps. Organizations should also reorganize and
centralize knowledge in hybrid work, so that remote
and hybrid workers can easily find the data they need
to do their jobs efficiently. Successful hybrid teams
must document processes such as recording

information in a central place and make it available to everyone. Creating virtual workplaces is another great way to share information; many tools such as Microsoft Teams offer virtual workplaces for teams to spend time together and share information as if they were in the same office. Managers should promote regular training, pairing team members from different departments and mentoring schemes: training and pairing employees promotes knowledge sharing. Finally, managers should also promote an information-sharing culture by sharing what they know often, encouraging their team members to share knowledge, and discouraging information hoarding.

- **Unconscious bias and the two-tier workforce**
    Hybrid work is still a relatively new way of working and for many workers, it is unfamiliar and different to what they have experienced before. As a result, the majority of employees, including leaders and team leaders, hold some degree of unconscious bias towards hybrid work and towards hybrid and remote workers. Many believe unconsciously that hybrid work hinders employee experience, that it makes hybrid workers less productive, and even less innovative. Many managers I have worked with believe that remote workers and hybrid workers are simply not as committed to their job as their office colleagues. For some managers, this belief is very conscious and openly shared; for others, this belief is unconscious and implicit – this is when proximity bias and distance bias come into play.
    In order to avoid creating a two-tier workforce that is unfair and to prevent unconscious bias towards hybrid and remote workers, organizations can follow a

Some managers unconsciously favour employees who are closer to them physically (in the office with them) over employees who are further from them physically (remote employees). In the long term, this can lead to the unintentional creation of a two-tier workforce: one workforce that is in the office, that gets promoted, recognised, and receives mentoring and career advancement opportunities; and another workforce that is remote, that misses out on promotions, pay rises, career progression, and recognition.

few simple strategies. First, organizations should invest in training and development for managers of hybrid teams. Most managers have never been taught how to manage a hybrid team, so by training them and giving them the tools to do so, organizations remove the risk of unconscious bias. Organizations should also survey their employees on their perceptions and experiences of proximity bias. Questions should include, for example: Have you been impacted by proximity bias? If so, how? Do you believe that office workers are favoured over remote workers? Do you believe that you or your colleagues have been treated differently because of where you work from? Leaders should also revisit their workplace policies and processes to ensure there is no bias towards in-person workers. Many workplace policies were written decades ago and have not been revisited since hybrid and flexible work have become more common. Companies should also educate employees to discuss unconscious bias, proximity bias, and distance bias by sharing educational resources, holding company town hall meetings about this topic, and planning training sessions about unconscious bias during the year. Finally, by monitoring feedback and surveying employees throughout the year, organizations can mitigate the risk of unconscious bias coming into play.

- **Employee engagement and camaraderie**

    Since the Covid-19 pandemic and the introduction of remote and hybrid work, many research papers have revealed how employees feel more disengaged and less connected than in office environments. According to a poll of over 2000 employers and employees from all around the world that was published in the *Harvard Business Review*, as many as two-thirds of employees who work remotely are not engaged in their work. The poll also discovered that employees who work outside of the office are less likely to remain with their companies for the long haul.[13] Feelings of connection and belonging are key to retaining employees and they should be intentionally nurtured in a hybrid work environment, where opportunities for spontaneous and organic communication are less frequent than in a traditional office environment.

    Leaders can implement a few strategies to foster employee engagement and camaraderie in a hybrid work environment. First, Leaders can also identify 'culture champions' in their own teams; recognising 'super connectors' and allowing them to drive employee engagement programmes can significantly improve employee leaders should focus on creating opportunities for connection among employees, more so than in a traditional office environment. By hosting virtual lunches, facilitating mentoring programmes, pairing remote employees with office employees, and creating employee resource groups (ERGs), organizations can foster greater connection between employees. Second, leaders can learn how to be more empathetic; they can learn to listen and learn more effectively. By paying more attention to feedback in their one-to-one meetings with employees, sending out more frequent surveys, and discussing survey feedback with employees, leaders can truly connect with their employees in hybrid work.

engagement and camaraderie in the hybrid workplace. Finally, fostering celebration is a great way to boost camaraderie in hybrid work; acknowledging small and big wins and recognizing success is a powerful way to bring teams together around their success. Creating a culture that celebrates career achievements, anniversaries, and even personal life events is a great way to bring the team together in a positive way and to create rapport and connection opportunities.

Hybrid work can still present some challenges for managers and organizations at large, especially for managers who are relatively new to leading hybrid teams and who might hold some unconscious bias towards in-person work.

Some organizations have tried to shift to hybrid and remote work, and failed, like in the cases of

Reddit and Yahoo, mostly because they didn't prepare and plan for a successful hybrid work environment. Luckily, there are practical ways for leaders and managers to mitigate the risks related to hybrid work. As American author and leadership expert Jocko Willink said, 'Leading people is the most challenging and, therefore, the most gratifying undertaking of all human endeavors.'

Checklist for the Four-Pillar Framework

The main goal of this book is to provide leaders with a guide to successfully build, retain, and develop a thriving team in a hybrid work environment. Throughout this book, I have shared a variety of strategies to do that, by using the four-pillar framework that I have developed and refined throughout my years of consulting with organizations. Although I have done my very best to make this four-pillar framework as simple and straightforward as possible, I realize that it covers a lot of concepts and that it may be time-consuming to go back to it and search for information quickly. This is why I want to share with you a practical checklist that you can use 'on the go' and easily go back to when you need a refresher. I have used the same four-pillar framework, and I have added a handy list of items to check and ensure that you are on the right track. The best way to use this checklist is to simply write down each item listed on a blank sheet of paper and to honestly write down where you stand next to each item. You will be able to easily identify areas where you are doing well already as well as areas for improvement. Here goes:

Pillar I: Create a Unified Hybrid Leadership Team

1. **Using values to unify**

   ◆ I articulate who, in my leadership team, is involved in the process of identifying company values.

   ◆ I get full commitment and buy-in from the leadership team on company values.

   ◆ I encourage my leadership team to research inspiring core values.

   ◆ I consolidate company values with my management team to integrate the ones that resonate most.

Figure A.2   Pillar I – Create a unified hybrid leadership team.

2. Role-modelling and setting the tone

- I build trust by refraining from rushing to fix things; instead, I allow my team members to think through challenges themselves.

- I build trust by saying when I don't know.

- I adopt a positive attitude by being mindful about how much time is spent with negative co-workers.

- I adopt a positive attitude by choosing positive language and becoming more conscious of the words being used.

- I adopt a positive attitude by being nice to colleagues.

- I inspire my team by setting a clear goal for my leadership team to inspire their team.

- I inspire my team by offering personal and professional development opportunities, encouraging continuous learning (online or face-to-face), normalizing feedback, and encouraging knowledge sharing.

- I inspire my team by sending regular pulse surveys asking for feedback and taking action on the feedback shared with me.

- I inspire my team by exhibiting integrity and by conveying the importance of integrity within my leadership team.

- I inspire my team by exhibiting integrity and by asking my management team: 'What makes integrity important in our organization?' 'How will integrity allow you to do your best work?' 'Who do you need to work with to exhibit high levels of integrity?'

3. **Setting common goals**

- I identify business goals for my leadership team by facilitating the process and letting my leaders contribute so that they feel emotionally involved in the goals.

- I ensure that my leadership team comes up with their own common goals because it creates accountability and ownership within my team, and it will keep team members aligned towards a shared objective.

- I pose the following questions to my leadership team to help them set common goals: 'What does our company/team/business unit stand for? What are our values?' 'What is the reason the company/team/business unit was created?' 'Where do we want the company/team/business unit to be in 10 years, in 20 years and in 30 years?' 'What is one goal that will never be compromised for other goals? In other words, what value is more important than any other value in our company/team/business unit?'

- I help my leadership team set SMART team goals (Specific, Measurable, Achievable, Realistic and Timely) because I understand that when my leadership team do this they are much more likely to focus their efforts and achieve their goal.

- I ask my leadership team the following questions to help them set specific SMART team goals: 'Are our team goals specific enough?' 'Are our team goals measurable? If so, how will we measure our goals?' 'Are our team goals achievable?' 'Are our team goals realistic?' 'Do our team goals have a timeline associated with them?'

- I shared with my leadership team some examples of SMART team goals.

- I make sure that my SMART team goals are aligned with the business goals that have been previously identified by our team.

- I document team goals because I understand that writing down goals increases the likelihood of achieving them.

- I ask each of my leaders to write down the team goals in their strategy and to share their strategy with each other.

- I encourage my team to use active words such as, 'We will increase our customer NPS to 90% within the next 6 months across all geographies.'

- I don't have just one leader solely accountable for a team goal; I ensure that every leader plays an active role for each team goal by articulating how each leader will play a role for each goal.

- I am specific and clear about what success looks like.

- I ensure that each team goal is connected to the business goals and the organization's values.

- I measure progress on team goals through frequent check-ins and ensure that progress tracking is part of our regular meetings agenda.

4. **Creating opportunities to co-lead**

- I match leaders intentionally for co-leadership projects by thinking about the outcome and asking questions such as, 'What am I hoping to achieve with this co-leadership team?' 'What result do I wish to

get with this specific team of leaders?' 'How will this
co-leadership further unify my leadership team?'

◆ If some of my leaders are not as aligned or as unified
as I want them to be, I consider asking them to
become a unit by inviting them to co-lead a specific
project together.

◆ I always consider matching leaders from departments
that do not usually interact because I understand that
these cross-functional, co-leadership teams will spark
creativity and innovation and open up new
collaborations that will further align my
leadership team.

◆ I monitor and facilitate the relationship between
co-leaders because I understand that co-leadership
projects will inevitably bring some conflicts. I know
that healthy conflict is actually essential for the
success of the organization because it allows everyone
to feel heard and valued, and it helps reach the best
outcome for the business.

◆ I expect conflict, and I tell my leaders to also expect
natural, healthy conflict during their co-leadership
journey to normalize healthy, productive conflict
within my leadership team.

◆ I encourage my co-leaders to establish some rules
that will help them reflect on their co-leadership
dynamics.

◆ I remind my co-leaders to ask for help when they
meet a roadblock.

◆ I remind co-leaders to define roles and
responsibilities.

- ◆ I encourage my co-leaders to be open and honest about who owns what and to keep each other accountable.

- ◆ I encourage my co-leaders to bring the fun into their co-leadership projects.

- ◆ I remind my team that co-leaders who are having the most fun in their projects are often those who also are the most successful with their projects.

5. **Scheduling informal time**

- ◆ I set up non-work-related spaces to better build rapport, trust, and positive feelings among my leadership team.

- ◆ I create Slack channels that are dedicated to non-work topics, including: pets, family, games, motivation, travel, weekend plans, etc., for my leadership team to encourage small talk and informal conversations between my leaders.

- ◆ I encourage the CEO, managing director, or the most senior person to be an active participant in these non-work-related Slack channels so that other leaders and employees will mirror their CEO's behaviour and share their own personal stories.

- ◆ I host virtual breakfasts, lunches, and coffee breaks, and I pick a day and time that suits most people by taking into consideration time zones or by rotating the time to make it fair for everyone in a dispersed team.

- ◆ I pay for my team lunches because it demonstrates that it is my organization/team/business unit who wants to facilitate social interactions between all colleagues, and because it also sends the message that my organization values time spent together socializing.

- I test the format of my virtual breakfasts, lunches, and coffee breaks and I let participants get involved.
- I host group learning sessions because I understand that leaders and employees will stay at the company longer if I invest in their career development. I recognize that learning and development sessions at work boost employee engagement and improve collaboration.

Pillar II: Build Extreme Transparency

1. **Attract and retain transparent people**
   - I check all candidates' references rigorously by posing open questions about the candidates to their previous employers and listening without interrupting.
   - I document everything so that I can go back to my notes if needed at a later stage.
   - I contact the references myself if I am the hiring manager, rather than using a third-party agency, because it's important that I speak with previous managers to get as much context and background as possible about my prospective employee.
   - I give candidates assessments to test their skills, work style, and experience before hiring because I understand that assessment tests are a great opportunity for me to assess how transparent the candidate is, based on the information they shared previously on the resume.

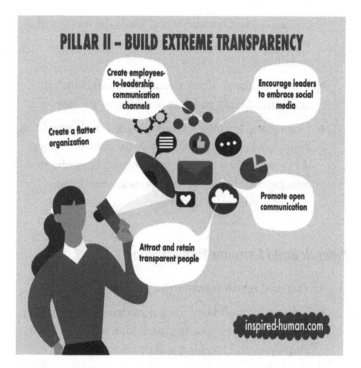

Figure A.3   Pillar II – Build extreme transparency.

- ◆ I research the candidates online to judge whether they are the candidate they claim to be on their resume because this will help establish how transparent and trustworthy they really are.

- ◆ I pay attention to a candidate's body language and tone of voice during the interview process because these can reveal a lot more about them than the words they use.

2. Encourage leaders to embrace social media

- ◆ I encourage my team leaders to embrace social media by sharing valuable information for our customers online because I understand that this will organically build trust with our customer base, and it will also build credibility and thought leadership.

◆ I encourage my team leaders to embrace social media by reading and responding to people's reactions online because I understand that social media is a two-way communication, and this will build engagement.

◆ I understand that connecting with customers online will also build brand loyalty, so by inviting my leaders to read users' comments and respond, it will demonstrate that we actually care about our customers and prospects.

◆ I invite my leaders to leverage social media by focusing on company culture because I understand the importance of engaging with employees' posts on social media.

◆ I encourage my team leaders to embrace social media by being authentic.

◆ I invite my leaders to leverage social media by sharing what they are comfortable sharing and building on it, because I understand that the more they share, the more natural it will become for them to share, and the more trust it will build with our community.

3. Promote open communication

◆ I host open meetings where all participants are encouraged to speak up and contribute.

◆ I often implement the round-robin method where each participant takes a turn to speak.

- I often appoint a dedicated meeting host to ensure that each participant gets equal speaking time.

- I foster open communication in hybrid work by limiting the use of chats during meetings because this can be very distracting and take the attention away from the presenter.

- I encourage meeting participants to speak up if they have any question or feedback during the meeting so that everyone can hear them and focus on what is being said rather than being distracted by the chat conversation.

- I prioritize networking as often as possible to foster open communication.

- I often start meetings with some icebreaker questions for the participants.

- Wherever possible, I try to schedule some networking and team-building time face-to-face as this is the most powerful way to build rapport. If face-to-face team-building is not possible, I host virtual networking meetings.

- I do frequent check-ins with my team, and I practise an open-door policy.

- I send emails to my team to say that I am available at specific times for catch-ups to encourage people to call me and discuss any topic they want to.

- I invite people to add colleagues during meetings when needed to encourage an open-door policy in a virtual world.

4. Create a flatter organization

◆ I empower front-line employees to get involved with the leadership team.

◆ I create opportunities for front-line employees to speak directly with the leadership team.

◆ I host regular all-hands meetings that are hosted by individual contributors because this is a powerful way to achieve extreme transparency and to let information flow from employees who are 'on the ground'.

◆ I delegate decision-making to everyone because each employee is trusted to make the best decision for the organization, without any need to request approvals.

◆ I encourage everyone to become role models, even more than in an in-person environment.

◆ If I work in a hybrid work environment, I work as many days remotely as I do in the office, sending the message that I support a hybrid work environment.

◆ I encourage my senior managers to become inspirational leaders and to lift people up by celebrating employee empowerment.

◆ I invite leaders in my team to embrace opportunities to mentor some employees to show their support and availability.

◆ I lead through consensus because as the organization becomes flatter and as the team continues to be geographically distributed, it is important that leaders transition from a traditional 'command and control' leadership approach to a 'consensus-led' approach to leadership.

◆ I often ask open questions in team meetings; I listen and take notes.

5. **Create employee-to-leadership communication channels**

   ◆ I support two-way communication between the leadership team and employees.

   ◆ I host long Q&A sessions in my weekly town hall meeting, and I host special Q&A sessions based on the feedback I received in previous town halls to show that I listen and that I care, and I want to continue the discussion.

   ◆ I proactively ask for feedback, and I act upon it.

   ◆ I make information accessible to every employee, in a way that makes it easy for employees to find where the information is.

   ◆ I foster a culture of authenticity to build trust in a hybrid work environment.

   ◆ I understand that authentic leaders who communicate often to all employees build more trust and transparency in the organization and set the tone for what type of relationships they want to see in their organizations.

   ◆ I measure employee engagement in order to adjust the communication channels.

Pillar III: Overcommunicate Through All Channels

1. **Assess your communication channels**

   ◆ I survey employee engagement by sending a monthly pulse survey focusing on communication. I make sure that this survey is anonymous so that employees feel safe to voice their concerns and ideas in a secure

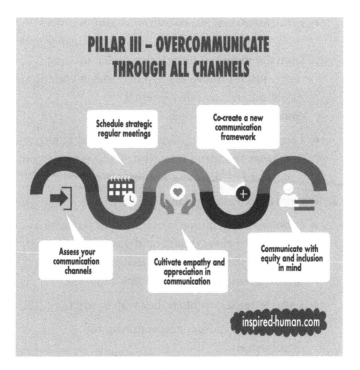

Figure A.4 Pillar III – Overcommunicate through all channels.

environment. I also analyse results based on the employee working style: the responses from fully remote employees might differ from the responses of the fully office-based employees, which might also differ from the hybrid employees.

- ◆ I host focus groups to discuss communication channels. I take the time to collect qualitative feedback to understand the real challenges and opportunities related to communication in hybrid work.

- ◆ I study performance data from communication tools and technologies, including performance data from the monthly internal newsletter, intranet usage, instant messaging app, monthly all-hands Zoom call, or any other internal communication channel.

- ◆ I pay attention to employee turnover, and I hold exit interviews and spend time with employees leaving to understand their reasons for leaving.

2. **Schedule strategic regular meetings**

- ◆ I choose the right meeting cadence for my team to decide whether we should hold quarterly meetings, monthly meetings, weekly meetings, or daily meetings, based on their feedback and need.

- ◆ I ask my team how often they wish to meet.

- ◆ I set up some cadence meetings with my direct reports.

- ◆ I ensure that I don't cancel one-to-one meetings without rescheduling because it will be more difficult to build trust, inclusion, and belonging in a hybrid work setting if I frequently cancel important cadence meetings.

- ◆ I set up cadence meetings with the team because I understand that teams really come together when they meet.

- ◆ I pay attention to the time allocated versus the time actually spent in team meetings.

- ◆ I focus on team morale and engagement at work because this is a great indicator of the effectiveness of my team meetings.

♦ I frequently ask myself if the people in the meeting are the right meeting participants and if some of them should be in separate meetings, and I do an audit of my meeting agenda.

3. **Cultivate empathy and appreciation in communication**

♦ I acknowledge and compliment employees' work when necessary, especially remote workers and hybrid workers who could often feel that their hard work is not being recognized as much as their office-based counterparts.

♦ I understand that people working in positive environments where praising is common practice are more likely to praise their co-workers' work, which in turn, creates a virtuous cycle of praise, appreciation, and empathy.

♦ I encourage managers to show their appreciation of their hybrid team by offering rewards.

♦ I often ask for feedback about work, workload, and progress, as well as about work-life balance, any need or help, or anything else that the employee feels is important.

♦ I take time to build trust and rapport with each and every one of my colleagues before asking for feedback.

♦ I build rapport with my colleagues every day by checking in often, asking open questions, and practising active listening.

♦ I leverage technology to collect feedback by sending monthly employee pulse surveys to gather quantitative feedback.

- ◆ I support flexible work by becoming a vocal advocate of flexible work.

- ◆ I often talk about my support for flexible work during team meetings, one-to-one check-ins, and any company all-hands meetings.

- ◆ I often ask my team members and co-workers how they feel about their current working environment, and I listen to their requests.

- ◆ I always seek to find out if any of my team members are going through a challenging time and might need special working arrangements to demonstrate empathy and to nurture a culture of camaraderie and support, which is fundamental in a hybrid workplace.

4. **Co-create a new communication framework**

- ◆ I identify and articulate new engagement rules in hybrid work because I understand that communication is more asynchronous than in an office setting, that employee distractions from work are more frequent (family members, kids, pets, deliveries, etc.), and that it is more challenging to achieve a sense of familiarity between employees organically.

- ◆ I ask my colleagues how they want to engage with each other, what channels they prefer to use for each project, and how they want to share information in a way that is productive and mindful of everyone's work preferences.

- ◆ I do not assume that my own personal preferences are the same as my team members' and ask my team how and when they want to collaborate.

- Once I have identified how my team likes to collaborate, I write down these rules of engagement, and I share them with the wider organization and make them accessible to everyone.

- I revisit our rules of engagement regularly as new team members join the team and as new needs and trends arise, to refresh them and keep them current.

- I document processes and technology to improve collaboration, especially for new starters who are not familiar with the systems and the team.

- I discuss with my team members what they would like to document in relation to communication guidelines.

- I write a handbook for my team on how to communicate in a hybrid work setting and share this handbook with new starters and the wider organization.

- I organize office working days by allowing employees to decide how often they want to meet in-person, where they want to meet in-person, and what format they prefer for a face-to-face gathering.

- I ask colleagues what works for them and how I can facilitate in-person meetings, I invite all employees to contribute to the discussion, and I listen to what is being said.

- I involve people in organizing in-person office working days to build a more participative approach to communication in my team.

- I schedule time for frequent improvements for my team's communication framework.

◆ I discuss with my team members how often we should revisit our communication framework.

◆ I often ask my colleagues when they would like to refresh the team's communication guidelines and tools to adjust to their changing needs.

5. **Communicate with equity and inclusion in mind**

◆ I make a point to over communicate with all employees in order to make everyone feel included and part of the team.

◆ I replicate informal office interactions.

◆ I send weekly emails to my team, I host informal chats with remote employees, I encourage pre- and post-meeting socializing, I hold company-wide meetings to sync up, and I highlight my team's success internally.

◆ I refresh my internal communication channels and also help create more inclusion and equity between remote employees and office employees.

◆ I describe explicitly which channels should be used for various types of communications (email, chat apps, meetings, etc.).

◆ I encourage more inclusive practices such as choosing to use group email threads where project discussions are visible to everyone rather than one-to-one emails.

◆ I ensure equitable practices by reviewing workplace practices and policies, as they might hold hidden bias towards in-person workers, giving them an unfair advantage.

- ◆ I focus on results-based performance rather than office-presence evaluations to ensure that remote workers are assessed fairly.

- ◆ I am intentionally transparent about the principles used to determine who gets promoted, who gets recognition, who gets new projects, who gets new assignments, etc.

- ◆ I hold people accountable to create a culture where a sense of fairness is pervasive.

- ◆ I monitor feedback closely to recognize the needs of remote workers.

- ◆ I talk openly with my team, acknowledging the issues that hybrid work can bring and hosting team meetings to discuss hybrid work.

- ◆ I organize team-building activities such as a group walk 'n' talk.

- ◆ I start a unique conversation by creating a list of unique questions for my team.

Pillar IV: Unify Cross-Cultural Hybrid Teams Through Cultural Awareness

1. **Promote psychological safety and inclusion**
   - ◆ I set the tone and lead the way because I understand that, in a virtual-first work environment, employees look up to their team leader, managers, and leadership team more than in a traditional office setting for direction on how to behave.

Figure A.5   Pillar IV – Unify cross-cultural hybrid teams through cultural awareness.

- ◆ I am willing to be vulnerable and model that it is acceptable to make mistakes, in order to build psychological safety.

- ◆ I frequently say thank you to people sharing opinions and using a direct and respectful style of communication.

- ◆ I challenge assumptions, and I commit fully once decisions are made and respond positively to challenges.

◆ I share positive examples of successful organizations that have achieved amazing success based on their focus on psychological safety, to help convince my team that they should try it.

◆ I help people connect by facilitating conversations that are focused on building connections, rapport, and camaraderie between team members.

◆ I host meetings to discuss everyone's hobbies, favourite holiday destinations, and interests outside of work. I create Slack channels for my team to discuss personal news and hobbies. I start an Employee Resource Group about common interests in my team.

◆ I create a space for my team members to share their personal interests and to help them connect and create more psychological safety in my hybrid team.

◆ I am vigilant, and I watch out for harmful comments.

◆ I pay extra attention to seemingly harmless comments from team members such as, 'you should already know this, we already talked about it last week', 'you should be familiar with that process since you have been here six months', or 'we already discussed that and decided what to do so there is no need to debate it anymore'.

2. Create a cross-cultural awareness programme

◆ I plan for success before I start implementing any cross-cultural awareness programme, and I consider how much my team is already going through.

- I find ways to get my team excited about a cross-cultural awareness programme so that they are interested and fully embrace it.

- I ask my team what they would like to learn about each other's cultures.

- I share examples of successful teams that have embraced cultural diversity awareness and that have become twice as productive as a result.

- I explain why I believe that cultural awareness in our team will help everyone better understand each other and communicate in a hybrid work environment.

- I leverage existing channels and regular meetings to facilitate this cultural awareness programme.

- I use storytelling as a way to communicate about cultural awareness because stories are universal, and they transcend cultures and individual backgrounds.

- I share anecdotes about cultural awareness to help increase employee engagement, because people respond to people and get inspired by other people they can connect with.

- I encourage employees to share their stories related to cultural awareness, without forcing them to do so.

- I prioritize culturally aware communication within my team.

- I become more aware of local colloquialisms and expressions, and I replace these informal ways of speaking with more standard ways of speaking to improve communication.

- I raise awareness about differences in communication styles by sharing examples.

♦ I understand that learning is a journey.

♦ I understand that we all have unconscious biases and we all communicate differently based on the culture we were raised in.

♦ I set the expectations with my team members that understanding cultural differences is a journey, not a destination.

♦ I set the tone that we are all in this together and are all here to learn and attract more interest and engagement from cultural awareness training.

3. **Consider language fluency and national communication norms**

♦ I take into consideration language training for my team.

♦ I understand that some of my employees might not understand all the idioms, expressions, and ways of saying things that are used by my native English speaking team members.

♦ I explain to my team that language training can improve understanding from all the non-native English speakers in our team.

♦ I use simple language, and I repeat myself often to establish the rule implicitly that others should do the same.

♦ I avoid using jargon, idioms, or complicated vocabulary when it's not necessary.

♦ I share the message that simplicity in language is key, especially when my team is hybrid, international, and distributed over different countries.

- ◆ I also use visuals that are universally understood in my presentations to convey my message clearly, such as infographics, charts, and pictures.

- ◆ I discuss cultural differences, and I show respect for other cultures.

- ◆ I talk about famous cultural holidays in the countries where my team members are from, to educate my team about different norms and traditions.

- ◆ I celebrate all the national holidays of the countries that my employees come from to create the opportunity for my team to spend some time together whilst learning about a colleague's country history and culture.

- ◆ I remind my team to show respect for other cultures and languages.

- ◆ I do not tolerate jokes about language skills, and I act as a role model for the rest of the team to create a more united environment.

4. **Address conflict immediately**

- ◆ When conflict arises in my team, I document the conflict and gather the facts.

- ◆ If there is a conflict, I contact each team member involved and have a conversation individually to gather information about the issue.

- ◆ I also explain to my team members what I have observed about the situation, and I ask open questions.

- ◆ When conflict or tension arises in my team, I acknowledge it and discuss it openly.

- ◆ I understand that in a hybrid work setting, many conflicts happen because long-standing issues have been unresolved due to managers not noticing them and/or not addressing them.

◆ I use existing regular team meetings to discuss any issue that needs to be addressed.

◆ Once I have acknowledged and discussed existing tensions in the team, I make a point to also celebrate team success to set the tone and encourage teamwork and collaboration.

◆ I sometimes also discuss team conflicts online on a Slack channel if many of the team members work remotely and in a different time zone, so that I can discuss the issue more quickly than waiting to arrange a meeting.

◆ I set some ground rules and act as a role model in conflict resolution.

◆ I treat all my co-workers with respect and fairness. I listen to my colleagues' views, including if they are different from mine; when my view differs from my colleagues, I say so, and explain why.

◆ When I do or say something wrong, I apologize, and I encourage my team to do the same.

◆ I participate in open and constructive dialogue.

◆ I make a point to model the ground rules I set, to reinforce them and to send the message that I walk the walk.

◆ I track productivity, and I pay attention to small details because I understand that workplace conflicts cause stress, disruption, damage relationships, and affect employee morale and customer service.

◆ I pay attention to who remains quiet in meetings the entire time, and I notice if someone who used to come to the office often suddenly avoids the office and works from home all the time, because by paying attention to my team interactions, I am able to prevent conflicts before they arise or to address them as soon as they arise, avoiding escalations.

5. **Encourage team-building activities and build rapport**

- ◆ I hold regular non-work-related chats with my hybrid team because I understand that social interaction between colleagues, especially in a non-work-related context, significantly improves employees' well-being, engagement, and sense of belonging.

- ◆ I host a Friday 'weekend plans' Zoom call to talk about my team members' plans for the weekend. If possible, I make it more inviting by sending each of my team members a voucher to order their lunch at their desk so that people can share a virtual lunch together and talk about their hobbies, families, or interests outside of work.

- ◆ I host annual trips to exciting locations to foster very strong relationships in my team that would not otherwise be possible.

- ◆ During that annual team retreat, I schedule some team bonding activities and some free time for people to plan their own schedules as well.

- ◆ I incorporate cultural awareness in my team-building plan to increase the level of cultural awareness and to help my international team come together as 'one team'.

- ◆ I celebrate traditional holidays, national days, and food from the countries where some of my team members are from.

◆ I ask each team member to share a presentation on the norms, cultural standards, and habits of the country they are from, and how they differ from the country your company is headquartered to bring an element of cultural awareness into my team-building activities.

This checklist should serve as a practical guide for what to do to build, nurture, and retain a team in a hybrid work environment. Feel free to revisit that checklist as often as you wish to, and to score yourself for each item. You might notice that over time, your scores improve in some areas, which is a sign that you are becoming better at building inclusion in your hybrid team. Feel free to share that checklist with your colleagues, peers, and the rest of your organization. The more your colleagues will embrace that checklist, the more successful your team will become.

Endnotes

1. https://www.washingtonpost.com/ technology/2021/12/02/hybrid-work-video-calls/

2. https://www.nytimes.com/2021/11/16/business/ return-to-office-hybrid-work.html

3. https://hbr.org/sponsored/2021/07/addressing-the-biggest-challenges-of-hosting-hybrid-events

4. https://www.forbes.com/sites/ forbescommunicationscouncil/2021/01/04/ four-reasons-your-company-should-pivot-to-hybrid-events/?sh=7a1b88b944ce

5. https://www.ceo-review.com/over-50-of-remote-workers-are-worried-about-workplace-exclusion/

6. https://smallbiztrends.com/2019/04/remote-working-statistics.html

7. https://www.beroeinc.com/whitepaper/rise-of-hybrid-meetings-and-events/

8. https://www.ringcentral.com/us/en/blog/work-from-home-cancelled-lessons/

9. https://www.theguardian.com/technology/2013/feb/25/yahoo-chief-bans-working-home

10. https://www.peoplemanagement.co.uk/news/articles/two-thirds-of-employees-feel-less-connected-working-from-home#gref

11. https://www.forbes.com/sites/bryanrobinson/2021/11/01/new-research-shows-remote-and-hybrid-workers-suffering-physical-and-mental-health-dilemmas/?sh=6d6d2ec55aa9

12. https://www.cio.com/article/303928/keep-remote-and-hybrid-workers-engaged-with-access-to-knowledge-and-community.html

13. https://workingcapitalreview.com/2020/05/are-remote-employees-less-engaged/#:~:text=According%20to%20a%20poll%20of,anyone%20on%20their%20work%20team.

ADDITIONAL
RESOURCES

If you would like to have more information about how to create a successful team in a hybrid work environment, visit our website at www.inspired-human.com where you will find a range of resources including:

- The option to sign-up to our newsletter about tips and strategies to build, retain, and develop a successful team in hybrid work.
- Quizzes to assess your leadership skills.
- Video clips that describe some key concepts related to creating a successful team in hybrid work.
- Blog posts and articles with resources related to building a successful team in hybrid work.

Building, retaining, and developing a successful hybrid team is a journey that requires constant focus and effort. If you need help to execute any of the concepts discussed in this book, please contact us at Inspired Human: www.inspired-human.com.

ACKNOWLEDGEMENTS

I would like to thank my colleagues and friends at Inspired Human: Sampras Kayima, Lindsey Brown, Jillian Gan, Chris Pearson, Dan Barrowclough, Hazel-Jasmine Weller, and Gemma Adair, for their enthusiasm, energy, and daily support. Working with you every day is a joy, and I could not have come so far without your constant support, optimism, and talent. I want to acknowledge the work that you do at Inspired Human, and it is a privilege to work with you.

I want to thank my husband Matteo for his constant support throughout my book endeavours. His never-ending optimism, support, and encouragement have been absolutely priceless. Somehow, we both manage to develop our work-related activities whilst raising our two children without support and encouragement. I am forever grateful for my husband's motivation throughout all of life's challenges.

I want to thank my husband Matteo for his constant support throughout my book endeavours. His never-ending optimism, support, and encouragement have been absolutely priceless. Somehow, we both manage to develop our work-related activities whilst raising our two children, Manuel and Victoria.

I would like to also thank our customers at Inspired Human who trust us to grow their organization in a better way. Whether we are delivering a virtual workshop, a keynote session, facilitating a team building event, or providing advice, we always appreciate your faith in our services and it is always a great privilege to work for you and to watch your company grow stronger and better.

I want to thank my wonderful editor Syd Ganaden, Purvi Patel, and all their amazing colleagues at Wiley who have trusted me with this book and have always supported me since day one.

I thank my family and friends, especially my sister Alix-Anne, who has always believed in me more than I ever believed in myself, and also my brother Victor, my parents Florence and Dominique, and all my other relatives and friends who have always supported me.

ABOUT THE AUTHOR

Perrine Farque is the founder of Inspired Human, a diversity and inclusion agency specializing in helping organizations grow their business through diversity and inclusion programmes. Her passion for diversity and inclusion is reflected in her speaking, writing, and consulting. When she is not delivering keynote sessions, Perrine consults for CEOs and business leaders in how to leverage diversity to their competitive advantage. Perrine was nominated in the Top 50 Most Influential Women in UK Tech by *Computer Weekly,* and she is also a judge at the Diversity in Tech awards. The widespread interest in Perrine's principles have brought her to consult for a mix of Fortune 500 companies in the technology industry, manufacturing, telecommunications, retail, luxury, utilities, and financial services. She also speaks to thousands of business leaders each year at national and international conferences. Perrine lives in London with her husband, Matteo, and their two children Manuel and Victoria. To find out more about Perrine and Inspired Human, visit www.inspired-human.com/.

Perrine Farque is founder of Inspired Human, a diversity and inclusion agency specialized in helping organizations grow their business through diversity and inclusion programmes. Farque's passion for diversity and inclusion is reflected in her speaking, writing and consulting. When Farque is not delivering keynote sessions, she consults CEOs and business leaders in how to leverage diversity as their competitive advantage. Perrine was nominated in the Top 50 Most Influential Women in UK Tech by Computer Weekly and she is also a judge at the Diversity in Tech awards. The widespread interest in Farque's principles have brought her to consult for a mix of Fortune 500 companies in the technology industry, manufacturing, telecommunications, retail, luxury, utilities and financial services. Farque also speaks to thousands of business leaders each year at national and international conferences.

www.inspired-human.com

VISIT OUR WEBSITE:

Consulting	Speaking	Books
Workshops	Online courses	Free resources

INDEX

Page numbers followed by *f* refer to figures.